Hamdi's latest book *The Spacemaker's Guide to Big Change* is a call for a new way of doing things. Hamdi's work is relevant not only to planners and humanitarian workers but also artists and creative practitioners, who are looking for new ways to make a difference through their practice. Hamdi's belief in and focus on the everyday and ordinary, and the particular in people's lives, is a radical new starting point, that brings hope and empowers those of us who are ignored and overlooked.

Emma Chetcuti, Director, Multistory: a community arts organisation located in the Black Country in the West Midlands, UK

Hamdi is interested in activism and results. In this book he shows us how participatory practice can be a speculative as well as an integrative instrument in an inequitable world. These ideas, modes of engagement and insights are as relevant for intervening in our existing built environments as for imagining the sustainable form for places of human habitation in the future.

Rahul Mehrotra, Professor and Chair Department of Urban Planning and Design, Harvard University, USA

Both philosophical and practical, this reflective book contains insights that go beyond participatory practice. The collected cases, references, and wisdom unpack the challenge of making change in the face of complexity and competing voices, and give encouragement that we can start small, where it counts, now, to achieve desired futures.

Jamin Hegeman, Service Design Network

THE SPACEMAKER'S GUIDE TO BIG CHANGE

This book gives definition to participatory practice as a necessary form of activism in development planning for cities. It gives guidance on how practice can make space for big and lasting change and for new opportunities to be discovered. It points to ways of building synergy and negotiating our way in the social and political spaces 'in between' conventional and often competing ideals – public and private interests, top down and bottom up, formal and informal, the global agendas that outsiders promote and the local needs of insiders, for example. It offers guidance on process, designed to close gaps and converge worlds that we know have become divisive and discriminatory, working from the detail of everyday life in search of beginnings that count, building out and making meaningful locally, the abstractions of the global causes we champion – poverty alleviation, environmental sustainability, resilience.

Practice – the collective process by which decisions are negotiated, plans designed and actions taken in response to needs and aspirations, locally and globally – we see, is not just about being practical, but more. Its purpose is to give structure to our understanding of the order and disorder in our cities today, then to disturb that order when it has become inefficient or inequitable, even change it. It is to add moral value to morally questionable planning practice and so build 'a social economy for the satisfaction of human need'. Practice in these spaces 'in-between' redraws the boundaries of expectation of disciplinary work and offers a new high ground of moral purpose from which to be more creative, more integrated, more relevant, more resourceful – more strategic.

Nabeel Hamdi is currently Emeritus Professor at Oxford Brookes University. After qualifying at the Architectural Association in 1968, Nabeel worked for the Greater London Council, where his award-winning housing projects established his reputation in participatory design and planning. From 1981 to 1990 he was Associate Professor of Housing at MIT, where he was later awarded a Ford International Career Development Professorship. Nabeel won the UN-Habitat Scroll of Honour for his work on Community Action Planning in 1997. He founded the Masters course in Development Practice at Oxford Brookes, which was awarded the Queen's™ Anniversary Prize in 2001. Nabeel has consulted on participatory action planning and the upgrading of slums in cities to international development agencies, charities and NGOs worldwide.

EARTHSCAN TOOLS FOR COMMUNITY PLANNING SERIES

There is increasing global demand for more local involvement in the planning of the environment. This is the only way that communities will get the surroundings they want and make the transition towards a sustainable future. This series of short, accessibly priced, practical books has been written by the world's leading planning professionals to provide tools to support community planning wherever it occurs. Each book is a stand-alone, but together they create a compelling resource for planning professionals, community groups, activists, planning students and anyone looking to facilitate engagement in a community context.

The Spacemaker's Guide to Big Change
by *Nabeel Hamdi*
June 2014 |
Paperback |978-0-415-83856-9 | Hardback 978-0-415-83855-9 |
Ebook 978-1-315-77331-5

Community Matters
Edited by *Mallika Bose, Cheryl Doble, Paula Horrigan and Sigmund Shipp*
April 2014 |
Paperback 978-0-415-72387-9 |Hardback 978-0-415-72387-9 |
Ebook 978-1-315-84873-0

The Community Planning Handbook, Second Edition
by *Nick Wates*
February 2014 | Paperback 978-1-84407-490-7 |
Ebook 978-1-315-84871-6

Sustainable Communities
by *Rhonda Phillips, Bruce Seifer and Ed Antczak*
July 2013 | Paperback 978-0-415-82017-2 |
Hardback 978-0-415-82016-5 | Ebook 978-0-203-38121-2

The Placemaker's Guide to Building Community
by *Nabeel Hamdi*
April 2010 | Paperback 978-1-84407-803-5 |
Hardback 978-1-84407-802-8 | Ebook 978-1-84977-517-5

Creative Community Planning
by *Wendy Sarkissian, Dianna Hurford and Christine Wenman*
February 2010 |Paperback 978-1-84407-703-8 |
Hardback 978-1-84407-846-2 | Ebook 978-1-84977-473-4

Kitchen Table Sustainability
by *Wendy Sarkissian, Nancy Hofer, Yollanda Shore, Steph Vajda and Cathy Wilkinson*
November 2008 | Paperback 978-1-84407-614-7 |
Ebook 978-1-84977-179-5

The Community Planning Event Manual
by *Nick Wates*
August 2008 | Paperback 978-1-84407-492-1 |
Ebook 978-1-84977-293-8

The Community Planning Handbook
by *Nick Wates*
October 1999 | Paperback 978-1-85383-654-1 |
Ebook 978-1-84977-600-4

The Spacemaker's Guide to Big Change

Design and Improvisation in Development Practice

Nabeel Hamdi

First published 2014
by Routledge
2 Park Square, Milton Park, Abingdon, Oxon, OX14 4RN

and by Routledge
711 Third Avenue, New York, NY 10017

Routledge is an imprint of the Taylor & Francis Group, an informa business

© 2014 Nabeel Hamdi

The right of Nabeel Hamdi to be identified as author of this work has been asserted by him in accordance with sections 77 and 78 of the Copyright, Designs and Patents Act 1988.

All rights reserved. No part of this book may be reprinted or reproduced or utilised in any form or by any electronic, mechanical, or other means, now known or hereafter invented, including photocopying and recording, or in any information storage or retrieval system, without permission in writing from the publishers.

Trademark notice: Product or corporate names may be trademarks or registered trademarks, and are used only for identification and explanation without intent to infringe.

British Library Cataloguing in Publication Data
A catalogue record for this book is available from the British Library

Library of Congress Cataloging-in-Publication Data
A catalog record has been requested for this book

ISBN13: 978-0-415-83855-9 (hbk)
ISBN13: 978-0-415-83856-6 (pbk)
ISBN13: 978-1-315-77331-5 (ebk)

Typeset in Gill Sans & Janson
by Fish Books Ltd.

Printed and bound in Great Britain by
TJ International Ltd, Padstow, Cornwall

In memory of my parents, Zehra and Khalid
and of lost times in Baghdad

Contents

Illustrations	xiii
Acronyms and abbreviations	xiv
About the author	xv
Acknowledgements	xvi
Foreword	xvii
General Note	xx

Introduction	1

Part 1: Learning Practice — 5

1 Deciding on Purpose: In Search of Beginnings — 7
2 Learning and Practice: Understanding and Action — 13
3 Deciding How to Decide — 18
    Ways of Seeing: Looking and Listening — 18
    Ethics and Rationality — 23
    Disciplinary Work — 28
    Interdisciplinary Work — 33
    Narrative and Quality of Life — 36
4 Cross-cutting Themes: Ownership, Organization and Asset Building — 44
    Part 1 Summary: Things to Think About — 51

Part 2: The Spacemaker's Guide to Becoming Strategic — 55

5 Equity, Efficiency and Participation — 57
6 Equity, Efficiency and City Form — 65

7	Participation in Practice	75
	The Life and Organization of Place	75
	The Nature and Scope of Practice	77
	The Roles and Responsibilities of Practitioners	88
	Part 2 Summary: Things to Think About	92

Part 3: Country Files 95

	Introduction	97
8	Cultivating the Top: The Million Houses Programme of Sri Lanka	101
9	Case Files: Learning from Practice	108
	Navagamgoda	111
	The Missing Lightbulb	119
	The Living Room on the Landing	123
	The Tailor's Workshop	126
	Part 3 Summary: Things to Think About	134

Part 4: Enablement and the Art of Improvisation 137

	Introduction	139
10	Embracing Serendipity: Finding Opportunity in Ambiguity	140
11	'Yes is More:' Getting Unstuck: Working with Troublemakers	145
12	Insiders Out and Outsiders In: Practical Wisdom and the Co-Production of Knowledge	163
	Part 4 Summary: Things to Think About	170

Index 173

ILLUSTRATIONS

FIGURES

2.1	Looking for linkages	15
3.1	The mess of informality	18
3.2	The mess of formality	20
3.3	Smoke kills – deciding how to decide	26
3.4	'is' and 'does' – crossing boundaries	34
4.1	Buzzwords in other words	45
4.2	Everything is connected	46
4.3	No caption	49
9.1	Navagamgoda site planning options (1983)	112
9.1a	Cluster plan (1983)	112
9.2	Shell houses (1984)	113
9.3	Self-build (1985)	114
9.4	Site consolidation (1986)	114
9.5	Site consolidation (1986)	115
9.6	The restaurant house (1986)	115
9.7	Navagamgoda (2012)	116
9.8	Navagamgoda (2012)	118
9.9	The broken light fitting – public or private?	120
9.10	Broken railings – who maintains?	121
9.11	The living room on the landing: extension of flat	124
9.12	No caption	126
9.13	No caption	127
9.14	No caption	127
9.15	Playground or laundry space?	128
9.16	The tailor's workshop	130

TABLE

2.1	Divided agendas	14

ACRONYMS AND ABBREVIATIONS

ACHR	Asian Coalition for Housing Rights
CDC	community development council
CAP	Community Action Planning
FAO	Food and Agriculture Organization of the United Nations
GLC	Greater London Council
IDP	internally displaced people
MIT	Massachusetts Institute of Technology
NGO	non-government organization
NHDA	National Housing Development Authority
NTNU	Norwegian University of Science and Technology
PEAS	providing, enabling, adapting, sustaining
PSSHAK	Primary Systems Support Housing and Assembly Kits
RSA	Royal Society of Arts
SIGUS	Special Interest Group in Urban Settlement
UN	United Nations
UNDP	United Nations Development Programme

ABOUT THE AUTHOR

Nabeel Hamdi qualified at the Architectural Association in London in 1968. He worked for the Greater London Council between 1969 and 1978, where his award-winning housing projects established his reputation in participatory design and planning. From 1981 to 1990 he was Assistant, and then Associate Professor of Housing at the Massachusetts Institute of Technology where he was later awarded a Ford International Career Development Professorship.

In 1997 Nabeel won the UN-Habitat Scroll of Honour for his work on Community Action Planning. He founded the Masters course in Development Practice at Oxford Brookes University in 1992, which was awarded the Queen's Anniversary Prize for Higher and Further Education in 2001. He was awarded an Honorary Doctorate from the University of Pretoria, South Africa, in 2008. He was ARUP Fellow at the University of Cape Town and an Adjunct Professor at The National University of Technology, Trondheim, Norway. He is currently Professor Emeritus at Oxford Brookes University.

Nabeel has consulted on housing, participatory action planning and on the upgrading of slums in cities to all major international development agencies, and to charities and non-government organizations worldwide. He is the author of *The Placemaker's Guide to Building Community* (Earthscan, 2010), *Small Change* (Earthscan, 2004), *Housing without Houses* (IT Publications, 1995), co-author of *Making Micro Plans* (IT Publications, 1988) and *Action Planning for Cities* (John Wiley, 1997), and editor of the collected volumes *Educating for Real* (IT Publications, 1996) and *Urban Futures* (IT Publications, 2005).

ACKNOWLEDGEMENTS

As always, there are many who have contributed to the content and production of this book. In particular, I would like to thank Christine Chang for typing my near illegible manuscript and for the overall production and organisation of the text. K.A. Jayaratne (Jaya) for his introductions to people and organizations in Sri Lanka, for his ideas, editorial comments and generous hospitality. To Hans Skotte, for making our visits to Sri Lanka possible through his research funds at NTNU, awarded him for the study of post-war and post-crisis reconstruction. To Richard Simmons for his help in scanning my old slides – for clearing the skies from dust spots and making presentable for publication. To my wife Rachel for her design ideas, for her help in the production of illustrations and her advice and support throughout. To Viv Walker for printing copies for me to edit, and keeping me honest. Thanks also to Ryan Anderson for his initial ideas for cover design.

I would like to thank all those in the settlements of Colombo and the villages in Southern Sri Lanka for their time, insights and stories, which I have used liberally, in particular in Part 3 of this book. To friends and colleagues with whom I have brainstormed ideas, in particular in search of the title to this book, and for their feedback throughout.

Finally, thanks to Nicki Dennis and Alice Aldous at Routledge for their encouragement and positive feedback throughout.

Foreword

There are very few people who have made such a significant contribution to the art of pro-poor development practice in cities as Professor Nabeel Hamdi. In many different ways, he has pioneered the field of participatory and activist urban planning in international development work.

This new book continues Hamdi's path-breaking work and is more timely than ever. The poor majority is now the urban majority. They are living in fast-growing cities where stark contrasts of inequality are dramatically presented in built form. Dense urban populations are vulnerable to more frequent natural hazards and increasingly endemic violence. At such a time, the world of international development and humanitarian work is lucky to have so wise a guide as Hamdi to point the best way forwards.

Hamdi's approach has always drawn deeply from the intimate detail of people's lived experience. His is a very observant and compassionate activism. Iraqi by birth, Hamdi spent many of his childhood days in the busy streets of Cairo. Here he developed a keen eye for the minutiae of people's lives, and what they reveal about the much bigger networks, constraints and opportunities ranged around them. Famously small things from his earlier works like the bus stop, the pickle jar and the paint pots are revisited in this book. New ones like the leaky roof, the underground shop, the missing light bulb and Beryl's environmental map are added to great effect. Like icons, these small urban objects become the focus of an intense attention in Hamdi's work, and spawn a very practical reflection. There is meditation in his approach. The initial stillness of Hamdi's gaze as a practitioner is something from which we can all learn. His clear sight of the particular in people's lives becomes a starting point from which we must all act. The real genius of his seeing is the way he then joins up the small things with the big things, using detail to shape policy and practice. So, working with

Beryl, her map becomes the basis of an action plan with her city's planning office. The missing light bulb and its darkness expose the failures of property ownership in a Tsunami relief project and, ironically, shed light on new policies of title for its inhabitants.

Hamdi's developmental approach has always been highly creative, gently subversive and resolutely inclusive. He sees development as design in its most experimental and collaborative sense. Improvisation, adhocism, spontaneity and incrementalism are everything in Hamdi's method. Like research in fundamental chemistry, prodding about with minutiae leads you to small discoveries that yield large applications. Hamdi has always embraced paradox too: the way to go forwards is to work backwards; the best way to work high up at policy level is start low down at the individual level.

The creativity and relevance of this distinctly Hamdian approach is developed further in this new book. There is also a new emphasis on the ethics of this type of urban development work. Hamdi rightly argues that development practice needs to be grounded firmly in the moral intentions of respect and fairness. Everyone must be respected and included in development, and increased equity must be a perpetual criterion of development effectiveness. For him, the choices and strategies of participatory development are also best guided by a very conscious form of practical wisdom. This wisdom needs to deliberate judiciously across the four main aspects of Hamdi's methodology: providing, enabling, adapting and sustaining (PEAS). For Hamdi, like the witty graffiti on a bridge over the UK's MI motorway, the need to 'Give Peas a Chance' is an ethical call not just a good practice mnemonic. Working like this is the right thing to do.

This book speaks to emergencies as well as development. The current armed conflict in Syria has shown extraordinary new patterns of urban displacement and refuge. Many thousands of host-families are making new spaces for internally displaced peoples (IDPs) and refugees in their own homes. The number of school children in the Lebanese school system has increased by 50 per cent to accommodate Syrian children. Sadly, most internal armed conflicts now last for between 10 and 20 years, and result in similar new patterns of concentrated living. Increasing urban violence arising from gangs, organized crime and outlaw urban zones is spreading fast across parts of Latin America and even the USA. All these places require creative solutions. Hamdi's method of adding strategic value to small bits of practical work is ideally suited to the response phase of emergency operations. Rapid emergency shelter, cash distributions and house expansions to host IDPs can all become starting points for more strategic and sustainable improvements to urban living.

Hamdi's work has traditionally been read mainly by urban activists and planners. It now needs to be read by humanitarian workers, human rights activists, social entrepreneurs and politicians. This new book adds real value to Hamdi's earlier works: *Housing without Houses* (1995); *Action Planning for Cities* (1997); *Small Change* (2004) and *The Placemaker's Guide* (2010). This whole oeuvre needs to be embraced by people trying to address the urgent and growing needs of people living in poverty and danger in the world's urban spaces.

If urban violence represents a growing crisis in civil and political rights, the world's cities are also becoming the new locus for a crisis of social and economic rights. Dramatic levels of inequality between fast-growing middle classes and the sinking urban poor demand new models of urban planning, investment and opportunity. Natural hazards and environmental adaptation are also becoming central in urban politics and planning. Environmental risk management is now a strong focus for every town and city, as the tragic typhoon in the Philippines has recently shown.

In all these areas, Hamdi's work can help. It offers a very creative working culture and a specific methodology with which to meet the coming challenges in humanitarian and development work around urban disasters and violence. It is, therefore, my great pleasure to commend this book to everyone who has a role to play in making cities safer and fairer places, so making them into the 'kind of places they would like to grow up in.'

Dr Hugo Slim
Senior Research Fellow
Institute of Ethics, Law and Armed Conflict
University of Oxford

GENERAL NOTE

I have quoted from the following of my previous publications throughout this book:

Hamdi, N. (1991) *Housing Without Houses*. Van Nostrand Reinhold, New York and Practical Action Publishing (1995), Rugby.

Hamdi, N. (1996) (ed.) *Educating For Real: The Training of Professionals for Development Practice.* (Intermediate Technology Publications) Practical Action Publishing, Rugby.

Hamdi, N. and Goethert, R. (1997) *Action Planning for Cities: A Guide to Community Practice.* John Wiley & Sons, Chichester.

Hamdi, N. (2004) *Small Change: About the Art of Practice and the Limits of Planning in Cities.* Earthscan, London.

Hamdi, N. (2010) *The Placemaker's Guide to Building Community.* Earthscan, London.

All diagrams and illustrations are by the Author, unless otherwise indicated.

INTRODUCTION

This book gives definition to practice, in particular to participatory practice as a necessary form of activism in development planning for cities. It gives guidance on how practice can make space for big and lasting change and for new opportunities to be discovered. It points to ways of building synergy and negotiating our way in the social and political spaces in between conventional and often competing ideals – public and private interests, top down and bottom up, formal and informal, the global agendas that outsiders promote and the local needs of insiders, for example. It offers guidance on process, designed to close gaps and converge worlds that we know have become divisive and discriminatory, working from the detail of everyday life in search of beginnings that count, building out and making meaningful locally, the abstractions of the global causes we champion – poverty alleviation, environmental sustainability, resilience.

Practice – the collective process by which decisions are negotiated, plans designed and actions taken in response to needs and aspirations, locally and globally – we will see, is not just about being practical, but more. Its purpose is to give structure to our understanding of the order and disorder in our cities today, then to disturb that order when it has become inefficient or inequitable, even change it. It is to add moral value to morally questionable planning practice and so build 'a social economy for the satisfaction of human need.' It can rediscover the value of 'commons' and '…the collective power (needed) to reshape the processes of urbanisation.'[1] It enables us to cultivate afresh the ideals of planning and to reconceptualize fundamentally the planning process itself.

For practitioners seeking to safeguard careers and disciplinary identity in what some may see as the middle ground of anonymity, practice in these spaces in-between redraws the boundaries of expectation of disciplinary work and offers a new high ground of moral purpose from which to be more creative, more integrated, more relevant, more resourceful – more strategic.

This book gives definition to these ideals and to this form of activism in practice. It does this in four parts: in Part 1, Learning Practice, we see how our big purpose often blinds us to practical need and how practical need is often a good way to start building our big purpose, and in ways that are meaningful and appropriate. In deciding how to decide to intervene, I argue the importance of building our understanding of place and deciding our actions according to five progressively layered considerations: getting a sense of need and aspirations, of problems and opportunities by looking and listening; modifying our rationale for intervention based on ethical considerations and moral judgement; applying our disciplinary criteria in search of practical and often sector specific responses; expanding the value and adding opportunity to disciplinary work through interdisciplinary work; through narrative or other media, standing back from the detail and adding experiential value – what would it take for example to make it all 'a wonderful place to grow up in.'[2] Part 1 concludes by considering a number of cross-cutting themes that are key to the success and sustainability of programmes, and constructed as a model with participation as its binding characteristic, which I consider useful for the design, planning and evaluation of programmes and projects.

Part 2, Becoming Strategic, gives definition to participation and argues its value for achieving both equity and efficiency in development planning in cities. It gives context to practice profiling some of the key issues we face in relationship to both the equity and efficiency of urban management and city life. The impact on practice is profiled in three ways, an updated summary of the theories and principles explored in *Small Change*, *The Placemaker's Guide* and recent writings. First, looking again at the life and organization of place arguing the need to craft a careful balance between the structures we design and those we enable to emerge – between freedom and order, local organizations and urban, national and even global ones. Second we review the changing scope and purpose of practice, in particular ways in which practice can become more strategic, triggering positive change, dealing with some of the primary causes of problems, not just symptoms, managing constraints, going to scale, for example. Third we reflect again on the nature of professional interventions that all of this entails and the changing roles and responsibilities of practitioners using the PEAS model – what is it we should Provide and how much, what does it Enable, how will it change and be Adapted, how will it be Sustained?

Part 3, Country Files, looks first at what it takes to cultivate the political and policy environment starting at the top and so to create conditions for change, with Sri Lanka as our case study. What do the theories and principles explored in Part 2 mean when it comes to building enabling or support policies, specifically in this case for housing and urban development? How does one converge political ideals with practical realities, change mindsets, change habits and routines among the key government institutions? What kind of programmes emerged, how were these implemented and with whom? What kind of institutional reorganization did it all demand? Case Files evaluates a number of programmes, some which emerged from Sri Lanka's Million Houses Programme, some from post-Tsunami reconstruction in the same country using the model developed in Part 1 and draws lessons.

Part 4, Enablement and the Art of Improvisation, explores enablement and the value of improvisation. Through examples it illustrates what it takes to negotiate incrementally through a series of improvised workshops, a programme of work, how to work with troublemakers and decide priorities, what techniques might be useful and what role one plays in enabling these processes. In our final chapter we consider the skills and competencies needed to acquire prudence or practical wisdom, essential for enablement planning, getting insiders out and outsiders in, encouraging the peer group production of knowledge and building the knowledge commons.

My intent is that this book will be useful in various ways: in its anecdotal stories that illustrate principles and processes in our search for beginnings in project and programme design; in the ways in which practical interventions can be scaled up in size and impact and made more strategic; in the structure of each part that illustrates process and offers things to think about when deciding interventions (Parts 1 and 3), when elaborating the value of practice (Part 2), when cultivating an enabling policy environment (Part 3), when building programmes, negotiating priorities and working with troublemakers – when getting practical wisdom (Part 4). Throughout, this book offers ideas and techniques for teaching and training that might be useful in class work and fieldwork, which I believe to be transferrable because they are transformable, structured yet unprescriptive.

Finally for those like me who raid rather than read books I have provided short but detailed summaries at the end of each part. These can be copied and combined as a single handout, summarizing the essence of the book for students and trainees.

NOTES

1 Harvey, D (2012) *Rebel Cities: From the Right to the City to the Urban Revolution*, Verso, London.
2 See: Ward, C. (1996) *Talking to Architects*, Freedom Press, London.

PART I:
LEARNING PRACTICE

If you can't explain it simply, then you haven't understood it well enough.
                                                                A. Einstein

Source: Peter Liversidge, 2012, Yorkshire Sculpture Park

1

DECIDING ON PURPOSE:
IN SEARCH OF BEGINNINGS

On 27 July 2012, after completing my presentation at a conference I was attending in Glasgow, I was asked a question from the floor that I had thought that by now I was well practiced to answer: what is a development practitioner?

My strapline response should have been in two parts: first, my take on the ideals of development, which are: to release the potential for human endeavours latent in the everyday; to build new futures, reminding ourselves that all too often, poverty 'annihilates the future,'[1] and that the loss of hope adds fuel to the flames of social disruption and political extremism.[2] Dealing with poverty in all its multifaceted dimensions and all the inequalities in both the distribution of opportunity and the distribution of gain – however they are achieved – is therefore central to development work – central to the wellbeing of all.

Second, on what I have come to expect of development practitioners in skills, competencies and ambitions: a development practitioner is someone who can deliver practical solutions now, and sometimes in crisis or otherwise urgent settings, and at the same time makes space for progressive and sustained social economic development over the longer term. In this sense, they are the spacemakers to whom I refer in the title of this book, whether they be planners, artists, architects, engineers, health workers, social scientists, teachers or others involved in humanitarian work. You need prudence, a good measure of practical wisdom, entrepreneurship, flexibility and respect. You need the skills and competencies to be able to work within that 'sliver of sanity' in between formal and informal organizations, top-down or bottom-up, equity and efficiency. Most of all, you need the moral high ground from which to argue your cause and guide your decisions – which liberate you to work with the bad guys, the troublemakers, the power-holders – at all levels.

I might have gone on to suggest that the practitioner's art in development is analogous to the art of 'ready made.' It seeks to reposition and more, transform the ordinary in a way that makes it special, gives it dignity – a reincarnation of familiarity, making significant the seemingly insignificant, finding opportunity in the chaos and often oppressive conditions of poverty. Instead, my response was first to sketch out some of the big issues that define our purpose and give context to our work, nourished with some of those blinding statistics designed to provoke and engage. I started by outlining the inequities of globalization, fueled often by the contradictions in development objectives, between the moral obligation for equity and the economic imperative to attract investment and enhance productivity. I pointed to the 2 billion or more people from around the world who are poor or otherwise vulnerable, earn less than US$2 a day, stuck at the bottom of the development pile, suffering exclusion from the mainstream for political, ethnic, economic or other reasons. Their identity and sense of belonging to anywhere has long been undermined by the processes of urbanization and by the progressive and ongoing threat of eviction of the hundred of thousands who get in the way of development.

Then there are the impacts of conflict and climate change, in particular on the displaced – all the biases among aid agencies, some who allocate aid according to need (which might wind up financing the military) and some according to effectiveness to promote growth, 'which ends up (often) going to those with less need.'[3]

I found myself sketching out a world of problems that would be impossible to engage with effectively, given their scope and complexity, inducing as much guilt and hopelessness in knowing how to decide how to respond. And yet, oddly enough, the bigger and more complex the issues, the more blinding the statistics, the more worthy I felt my cause. By the time I was ready to answer the question, most had turned off or nodded off.

In my presentation, I had done what I thought I had learnt not to do in professional work. First, I had distanced most in the room from things that matter to them, starting as I did with my own agenda of issues, with what you should do, irrespective of who you are, rather than what you can or want to do. I was implying the kind of convergence between who you are and the world out there, which often 'causes the inner self to atrophy.' As Michael Foley notes in his book *Embracing the Ordinary*, 'it is as easy to lose the self in the world as it is to lose the world in the self.' What we need is to carefully balance involvement and detachment – 'the necessity of being both in and out of the game,' with careful attention to context.[4]

Second, and as a result, I had distanced myself from my public and in the manner and sequence of my presentation. I had sketched out the context before giving my answer, instead of giving my answer first, then giving context to how it was derived. I had assumed a certainty about the facts and about by my own convictions as to the order and disorder of the world I was encouraging my audience to engage with. 'But no one knows less than those who are certain of knowing everything. And no one is more dangerous than those who are convinced of knowing it all…Preaching and lecturing are usually futile because something in the listener always rebels against coercion.'[5]

Finally, I had devoted most of my response to profiling all the negatives of development, all the problems and disorder that give the professions the legitimacy to intervene and at a level and intensity that often suits outsiders more than insiders. We were in denial of the extraordinary resourcefulness that people bring while coping with, even solving, their own problems.

There have been times amid the hopelessness of it all when one stands back in search of something tangible, doable and immediately useful. Drop the big purpose and let's get the water running, the kids to school safely, the garbage picked up. And then you come to realize that these practical, more detailed interventions can be first steps to meeting bigger aspirations, because you come to realize as a development practitioner that you suspend rather than abandon your big purpose in order to get something going.

Giving bigger context to the detail enables the detail to contribute to the bigger context, to help shape the big purpose. If we have to fix the water, how can we do it to generate enterprise, empower minorities, improve accessibility, conserve supply, build community, save the environment? We look for catalysts, the least we need to do to get things going – the bus stop, the pickle jar, the school bus. We work backwards, asking progressively, what if? In so doing we distinguish ourselves as development practitioners, whatever our disciplinary backgrounds. We reach out for better futures, without losing the specificity of now.

I had come to this same conclusion some years ago when attending a community workshop in Peru. It was entitled 'Building Civil Society.' Its purpose was worthy and commendable, to give voice to local residents in processes that would enhance their wellbeing and build their resilience. The speaker was espousing his intent, and that of his organization, to empower civil society to engage with government to deliver better education, health services, housing – to democratize decision making and give people a say, as partners no less, in his schema of good governance.

Amid all the abstraction and good intent, one woman in the crowd spoke out. 'My roof is leaking, and like so many others who live here, we have no money or help to fix it.' But leaking roofs featured low on the speaker's priority list of issues, given his bigger purpose. He was there, after all, to promote the latest in World Bank strategy for poverty reduction at the time – expanding opportunity, empowerment, security. His response was polite, perfunctory and somewhat patronizing. We need first to conclude our discussions on empowerment, on democratizing decision making and on the importance of giving voice to an effective civil society, he said. We need a matrix of issues and actions with which to decide our respective responsibilities. We need a big plan. This will be the basis for deciding where to start, who can do what, who can help, when and how. It will be the basis for exploring new partnerships as we work toward our model of good governance. He had it all worked out. His reasoning was as if a light which had made him see things as they were not.[6]

The woman, who by now had even less idea what he was talking about, insisted on finishing her story. It was familiar to many and typical. She didn't want voice, she said, she wanted money and help, and wanted it now. With the absence of furniture in their house, they sit, sleep and cook on the floor, which is constantly damp during the rainy season. The kids get ill and miss out on school. The local clinic is usually crowded with people seeking help – it sometimes takes days to be seen and treated. They themselves get ill, miss out on work and struggle to meet their basic needs, paid as they are on a daily ad hoc basis. In the heavy rains last summer, a section of her roof collapsed, and the family moved in for a while with neighbours – the family was dispersed. Their insecurity is a constant stress on family life – because the roof always leaked.

As I listened to the dialogue and banter, I couldn't help but think: suspend your big purpose and fix the roof because by doing so, '...we learn about the structure of a problem by the process of solving it.'[7] Then do it in a way that feeds back into your big purpose. Reverse the cycle of survey, analyse, plan, implement and instead, get something going now, look to building this into the larger plan or purpose, do your analysis of what this will all entail in money, skills, capacities and the like, then do more surveys to figure out the root or primary causes of these symptoms, the long-term strategic agenda of programme and policies that may be needed city-wide.

In these ways, practical and strategic work go in parallel, not in sequence. The woman and her neighbours had identified a practical intervention that could have enormous collective and strategic value. The consequential linkages of her leaking roof and her inability to fix it herself invoke an immediate 'now' intervention that would improve health, lessen the burden on local clinics, give continuity of access to schools for children, lessen the stress on daily life and improve wellbeing. What if we were to organize collectively around house maintenance with skills, tools, materials and small grants that could be used to leverage additional support from local government once their credibility had been established? In this way, civil society would indeed have 'voice,' not only in deciding their needs, but also in negotiating other improvements – not least, security of tenure, making houses more flood resistant. And what if this could become a model for other areas city-wide, where communities would share knowledge and information, a network of community organizations might emerge that:

> *can begin to work at a city scale – for instance, gathering information needed to assess the scale and nature of citywide problems through citywide surveys. [These] networks or federations of urban poor groups come to be seen as viable development partners by local governments and other groups, so a platform for negotiation of partnership is built at city scale.*[8]

It would all be a start to building more resilient communities, an understandable and tangible way to empower and give voice.

NOTES

1. Orwell, George (1973) *Down and Out in Paris and London*, Penguin Modern Classics, Harmondsworth.
2. Albert Camus, with reference to the Algerian conflict, said 'in Algeria as elsewhere, terrorism can be explained by a lack of hope.' See *Algerian Chronicles* edited by Alice Kaplan, translated by Arthur Goldhammer, reviewed in *The Literary Review* May 2013.
3. Collier, P. (2008) *The Bottom Billion*, Oxford University Press, Oxford.
4. Foley, M. (2012) *Embracing the Ordinary: Lessons from the Champions of Everyday Life*, Simon & Schuster, London.
5. Foley, M. (2012) *Embracing the Ordinary: Lessons from the Champions of Everyday Life*, Simon & Schuster, London.
6. Picabia, F. (1986) *Who Knows*, Hanuman Books, Madras and New York.
7. Kay, J. (2011) *Obliquity*, Profile Books, London.
8. International Institute for Environment and Development (IIED) *Environment & Urbanisation*, Brief No. 26, October 2012: *Rethinking Finance for Development: The Asian Coalition for Community Action (ACCA)*.

2

LEARNING AND PRACTICE: UNDERSTANDING AND ACTION

Every academic year we start with a programme of self discovery, learning about the global themes that are important to us professionally, about our roles and responsibilities in the mess of practice, about converging learning with practice more effectively, about behaviour and the ideals and ethics that it takes to become a development practitioner. Most years there will be the usual rich mix of people from around the world, each with their own narrative of fact and fiction, good guys and bad guys, right and wrong. Each will have their own bias of guilt, for the state of the world placed squarely on one agency or another, one political system or another, one set of ideals versus another. Some will be aligned with government organizations, most with NGOs. There will be a mix of disciplines – architects, planners, engineers, others in health – some who are relief workers who themselves will have joined the relief and development business from a variety of backgrounds. The range of experience and status will vary considerably, an asset to be explored in learning, I have come to discover – and not a hindrance. Those with less or no experience will tend to be more imaginative, more creative, less clear on the rules and boundaries of what might be acceptable in the design of projects and programmes. They will therefore be more prepared to make up their own rules, to make mistakes and ask why not, less constrained by all of the people and politics that get in the way of change. The group will represent an extraordinary resource of knowledge, talent, cultural values, experience, which we are careful to socialize in search of difference in meaning and purpose. It is an exemplar of practice.

One thing at least we all share is a commitment to make the practical work we do, whatever our expertise, have lasting value in the context of the issues we choose to engage. We share a commitment for exploring new boundaries to our disciplinary core, so that we can remain rigorous to our discipline, but in ways that are relevant. We share a commitment, in other words, to becoming development practitioners – an ambition to become spacemakers.

I start our discussion on how best to close the gap between learning and practice, understanding and action. I provoke the group at first into believing that our choices today are 'either or'. Most will align themselves with the characteristics on the left side of Table 2.1, because most will have decided that to align yourself on the left is more tangible, more measureable in achievement, more safe.

Table 2.1 *Divided agendas*

Learning: Academic agendas	*Practice: Urban realities*
Institutional truths	Social/economic truths
Idealized goals (disciplinary)	Desired goals/needs (people)
Professional originality	Populist innovation
Experts as lead agents	Experts as catalysts
Understanding	Action
Policy making	Policy implementation
Rationalist thought/process	Informed intuition
Single disciplinary	Interdisciplinary/multidisciplinary
Specialists	Generalists
Single clients	Multiple clients
End states (projects)	Incremental/progressive (programmes)
Strict timetables	Open ended programme
Certainty/consistency	Uncertainty/transition/change
Big ambitions	Small beginnings

And then we debate complementarities between worlds, a more nuanced understanding of terms as a basis for convergence. We scramble the words (see Figure 2.1) and think again. We look for linkages.

An example is being a *lead agent* in *interdisciplinary* work that accommodates the *desired needs* of people, mobilizing all the resourcefulness and *innovation* latent in community. In this case, you are leading your profession out of its conventional silo and engaging with community. Similarly, exploring new partnerships between *multiple clients* with healthy competition demands significant

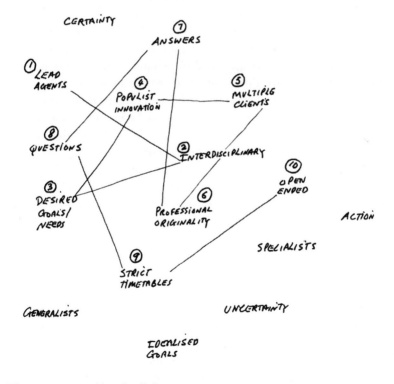

Figure 2.1 *Looking for linkages*

ingenuity and *professional originality*. Or, where the *answers* you got to difficult questions in one place invoke different *questions* about values and appropriateness in another place. Where *strict timetables* are essential to practical or 'now' interventions while at the same time recognizing the need for lasting, *open-ended*, strategic, more developmental responses.

All of this to get our heads straight, to develop a mindset, not in the linear, tidy reasoning of flow charts and bar charts but rather in the complex networked way of mindmaps. All this to explore new relationships and more synergy between understanding (inside) and action (outside). We debate for a while the gap between understanding and action and the way in which convention has it that first you need to know before you act. In these ways, understanding becomes progressively divorced from action as does research from practice and researcher from researched. Research then proceeds largely along reductionist lines, observation is strictly objective and its methods largely normative and hegemonic – that is, conclusions, models and laws are drawn up that assume universal value, and the observer assumes that he or she becomes the primary repository of that knowledge, which is then passed on, most times selectively, from those who have it to those who don't. Dependency and intellectual colonization are inevitable outcomes.

It doesn't take much following this sequential line of thinking to conclude, therefore, that good practice derives from good research, which then informs good policy. We now know that this is hopeful at best. Instead, I argue, good practice derives from good practice, where principles, methods and ideas can be tested, documented and constantly modified based on progressive reflection and learning, which Don Schon calls 'knowing in action.'[1] It derives from those who do it and think about it, passed on from generation to generation, passed across from one place, project or community to another, and passed up to governments, institutions, policy makers and academic researchers.

All of this in preparation for understanding more clearly not just what we see and why we see it the way we do, but also delving more deeply into what we're looking at and throughout, challenging our own professional roles, values and stereotypes as outsiders, which often interfere with lasting change.

NOTE

1   Schon, D.A. (1983) *The Reflective Practitioner: How Professionals Think in Action*, Basic Books, New York.

3

DECIDING HOW TO DECIDE

WAYS OF SEEING: LOOKING AND LISTENING

By now I had learnt not to start with the worthiness of our cause, not to blind everyone with numbers in our introductory session. And so we start with an image up on the screen (see Figure 3.1), a dense informal settlement or slum that can be anywhere. We start, in other words, in the street – on the ground.

Figure 3.1 *The mess of informality*

I ask everyone to stare deeply into the image and consider the following questions:

- What is public, what is private, what about privacy?
- What is front and what is back to houses?
- What about sanitation?
- What happens if there is a fire?
- What about transportation – how do the kids get to school?
- Where is the order and disorder?
- Who owns what? Who controls what?
- What happens when it rains?
- Where does the rubbish go? Who deals with it? Who pays for it?
- What about electricity? Who gets it from whom? Who pays what and to whom?
- What concept of community exists? What sense of belonging? Do people want to stay, or do they want out?
- What assets, tangible or intangible, exist? What aspirations?
- What kind of technology? Where is the ingenuity and innovation? Where is the resourcefulness?
- Who built it all and with whom?
- Do we see the place in the process of deterioration or consolidation?
- A place of hope or a place of despair?
- And then, how does this place work in relationship to adjoining areas? What is its place and legitimacy in the city as a whole?
- Where are its boundaries, both visible and invisible, and how might they be perceived?

Then we ask the same questions with respect to the contrasting image in Figure 3.2:

The purpose of our picture analysis is five-fold. First, to raise and brainstorm some key questions that will need to be informed in order to build our understanding of place. This will be a prelude to positioning our interventions. It will also be a basis to sorting out how best to conduct our transect walks. Second, to challenge one's

Figure 3.2 *The mess of formality*

own values and perceptions in the way we see these places, and to think again about whose values count, whose moral authority dominates. Third, to get into the habit of spotting clues which might lead lines of inquiry – physical clues, the flowerpots, the lines of laundry, the electricity pylons, the spare tires on the roofs – and clues in narratives not easily visible, which tell of experience and history, of networks and alliances. Fourth, to raise bigger questions about the place and value of informality and of formal planning in urban development and the kind of circumstances that lead to these kinds of settlements in the first place, whether planned or unplanned – questions of poverty, equity and sustainability and related planning policy. In all these respects, to emphasize from the outset the importance of understanding both visible and invisible structures of place, beginning to link symptoms of problems with causes, driven as they always are by the question, 'I see what I see very clearly, but what am I looking at?'

As we stare back into the image of the informal settlement (Figure 3.1), some will see it all, at best, as organized complexity, which they will distrust because they have been taught to see it as ugly, irrational, unauthorized, unmodelable, dangerous or even unfair. They will distrust the very processes that Jane Jacobs described as being 'of essence of city organization and life.'[1] In cities in developing countries and in our image on our wall, Jacobs could have been referring to all the entrepreneurs who speculate with land, provide services, work as moneylenders and manufacturers, as water vendors, garbage collectors and builders. Intricate and complex formal and informal partnerships develop for recycling garbage, purchasing and exchanging commodities, exerting political influence, pirating services and securing employment. In time, people build a substantial body of experience and knowledge that is rarely tapped when formulating plans about how best to build, to profit or to dodge the authorities. When things go wrong, no one needs to step in with elaborate explanations. People will usually know and will have the know-how, if not the means, to put it right. They will invent ways of working as they go, tailor-made to needs, aspirations, income and profit. The marketplace, both formal and informal, will have much to say about what happens, as will respected elders, tradition and local know-how. Indeed, recent research into 'conflict in cities and the contested state' concludes in one of its key findings: 'The informal and sometimes invisible fabric of practices that make everyday urban life possible must be better recognized as a resource for conflict management and resolution.'[2]

These informal practices we now know to be highly resourceful. They are resourceful because they are fast and ingenious and offer 'a vitality and energy of social interactions that depend critically upon diversity, intricacies and the capacity to handle the unexpected in controlled but creative ways.'[3] They are full of inventive surprises and highly productive. They are the essence of city organization – the lead agents of 'development.' 'Once one thinks about city processes, it follows that one must think of *catalysts* of these processes,'[4] removing barriers to learning, 'creating opportunities for discovery and a context for work which can be understood by all.'[5]

After some discussion, I bring us all up to date with a few numbers, and now in a way that is more meaningful. I remind everyone that by 2030, 4.9 billion people will live in cities and that over 1 billion people live in places similar to our picture, 56 million of them in developing countries. 'An estimated 1.57 billion people, more than 30 percent of the population of the 104 countries studied for the 2013 UN Human Development report, live in multidimensional poverty, that includes human deprivation in health, education and standard of living.'[6]

Then there is the rising tide of inequality, in cities, within nations and across nations. The United Nations Development Programme (UNDP) estimated that 53 countries in 2005, equivalent to some 80 per cent of the world's population, experienced rising inequality – in income, in opportunity and in the distribution of outcome.[7]

I ask everyone to imagine that the informal settlement that we are looking at in our image on the wall is India. For the poorest quartile of India's urban population, 60 per cent of children are not completely immunized, 54 per cent are stunted and 47 per cent are underweight; fewer than one fifth have piped water into their homes and fewer than half use a flush or pit toilet to dispose of the excrement.[8]

And then there is the threat of constant eviction and relocation, sometimes in the interest of 'beautification,' to attract investment, other times to salvage and restore World Heritage sites to attract tourists:

> *Since May 2006, more than 150 slums in Delhi have been demolished under government pretences of transforming India's capital into a clean and more cosmopolitan 'world city.' Home to the city's labourers and working class, slum colonies have come under increasing attack by politicians and more elite residents who criticize the spectre of poverty as leaving a black mark on the growing image of a 'shining India.' The slum demolition process has resulted in dire human rights violations of India's largest urban population, the working poor. Evicted from well-established squatter*

communities in the heart of the city, many poor families have been shipped out of sight.[9]

In Hampi (in Southern India), a World Heritage site of some 2000 monuments, some 326 residents catering to the needs of the tourists and pilgrims were evicted. 'Those with some savings have rented properties in nearby villages, others are staying with relatives. The rest...have been housed in rows of small huts built from bamboo and plastic sheeting on a patch of land outside the site perimeter fence.'[10]

Evictions are rampant everywhere – our image could be anywhere: 400,000 people evicted in Beijing in preparation for the Olympics, 700,000 in Zimbabwe's operation 'clean out.' In Cambodia, the government sale of land to foreign investors to develop its tourist industry displaced thousands, for example. And in Peru, on the eastern slopes of the Andes, the Pakitzapango hydroelectric dam, which could flood most of the Ene River valley, would likely displace thousands of indigenous Ashaninka people – all examples of the violence of development.[11]

ETHICS AND RATIONALITY

Given this context of issues and in our next phase of work, we consider the ethics of deciding our interventions. Given who we are as architects, planners, anthropologists, health workers, designers, economists, artists, mechanics or plumbers, how would we frame the issues and position our questions in response to the problems we believe we can and should engage locally and globally. How do we decide our priorities and with whom? And then, how do we decide where, how and with whom to intervene?

We stare back into the image of the informal settlement, and imagine again the woman with the leaking roof and the place in which she lives. Her narrative, which I complete, is telling. The woman's house is typical of many. The family of six lives there and the house has been extended over the years to accommodate their newly wedded son and the woman's brothers, who have been displaced from elsewhere, as well as their elderly mother. Despite cramped conditions, there is an abundance of home-based enterprise (some 50 per cent of the informal economy is home-based, and some 60 per cent of household income is generated by women). At the front of the house is a small shop, in the courtyard a collection of building materials – some for home use, others to sell on. In one back room doubling up as a bedroom is a small foot-pedalled sewing machine, a pile of clothes waiting for adjustment or repair. Others will rent rooms to new arrivals or as workshops. Cooking is on open fires in one room off the small courtyard. Fires in the settlement are common and difficult to control in the absence of fire-fighting services, and smoke, particularly in winter months, is a key hazard.

Sanitation is rudimentary. There are public latrines provided by the authorities but they are largely unusable. People defecate in the open walled-in yard in the back of disused latrines, which has been only recently segregated for men and women. Some NGO tried to promote an eco-latrine, easy to use in the home and which one puts out to be emptied by the authorities, but these were rarely collected. None have security of tenure and there have been occasional rumours of relocation to release the land for commercial development and middle-income housing, given the relatively central location. Twice they have been threatened with eviction. The stress on family life is constant. Despite the uncertainties, their house did represent a relatively substantial asset accumulated over time, added to incrementally, helping to reduce their physical vulnerability despite the leaking roof, and earning them additional income. It has helped to consolidate their household relations. They were not so much poor in income or even assets but rather, in capabilities, entitlements and rights. They were poor in opportunity and in their insecurity. They were poor in hope.[12]

In the absence of more detail, and as we consider our interventions, everyone in the room is encouraged to take positions guided by their own expertise, ideals and moral values, those of their disciplines or those of the organizations they were working for. The exercise gives us all a chance to profile some of the big issues that give context to informality and gets us to think, at first, about where we stand – what universal truths or principles are likely to guide our interventions, to decide right or wrong, good or bad, as outsiders. These kinds of ethical considerations give 'us a perspective for thinking and acting...[They] can improve our perspective and make it more reflective and better thought out.'[13] They guide the choices we make and helps decide what is appropriate, what is fair and efficient, given all the vested interests we confront, all the differences in priority among stakeholders.

I ask everyone to select a topic that they consider to be pertinent. Someone raises the issue, as an example, of cooking on open fires. Where do we stand on this subject? The group clusters into three textbook positions, at once reasonable and challengeable.

For one cluster, facts are facts. Cooking on open fires pollutes the environment, harms health, in particular the health of women and children, and kills. Theirs is the objective view, the moral realists whose decisions will be based on extensive survey and rigorous analysis gleaned universally and that leads one to state an objective or moral truth, confirmed by United Nations (UN) and World Bank statistics.

Indoor air pollution kills fifteen times more people living in poor countries than in rich ones. Each year, environment-related disease (respiratory, diarrhoea) kills at least 3 million children under five years of age – more than the entire under five population of Austria, Belgium, Holland, Portugal and Switzerland combined.[14]

According to the World Bank, 80 million women and children inhale smoke equivalent to smoking two packets of cigarettes a day; 60 per cent of female lung cancers in developing countries are among non-smokers; 2 to 5 million people suffer burns from kerosene lamps in India alone – with some 20 per cent of household income going to the purchase the kerosene.

One can conclude, therefore, that open fires (and kerosene lamps), particularly in dense urban areas, are wrong 'independently of what anyone may think or feel.'[15] For this cluster, reasoning leads one to ethical judgements. Amartya Sen, in his book *The Idea of Justice*, questions this basis of diagnosis:

> *Why should we accept that reason has to be the ultimate arbitrator of ethical beliefs? Is there some special role for reasoning, perhaps reasoning of a particular kind, that must be seen as overarching and crucial for ethical judgments? Since reasoned support can hardly be in itself a value giving quality, we have to ask, why precisely is reason support so critical? Can it be claimed that reason's scrutiny provides some kind of a guarantee of reaching the truth? This would be hard to maintain, not only because the nature of truth and moral and political beliefs is such a difficult subject, but mainly because the most rigorous of searches in ethics or in any other discipline could still fail.*[16]

Sen goes on to quote Hilary Putnam, 'real ethical questions are a species of practical question, and practical questions don't only involve valuings, they involve a complex mixture of philosophical beliefs, religious beliefs and factual beliefs as well.'[17]

Figure 3.3 *Smoke kills – deciding how to decide*

Sen and Putnam identify a second cluster, evident within our group, those who think that decisions on right or wrong, good or bad, cannot be absolute, whatever the facts and can only be decided relative to the cultural norms in which they exist. Morality, they argue, is a product of culture. Decisions on good or bad can only be decided in relation to what is socially acceptable. People are capable of weighing up trade-offs on money, habit and health – so long as they have choice. Indeed, 'people who speak of good or bad (right or wrong) as absolutes are absolutizing the norms of their own society. They take the norms that they were taught to be objective facts and impose them on others. Some things are not wrong, they say, just different.'[18]

And then there is a third cluster of opinion. The answer, they say, lies somewhere in between. I would call these the moral pragmatists, the development practitioners, looking to make space for change to happen. We can neither align ourselves to absolutes, whatever or however they are derived, nor entirely to relativism – not at least in a globalized world. For them, the first principle of aid is respect. Change has to be encouraged from within, through progressive adaptation, transforming habits and relationships through learning and awareness and by increasing choice. It cannot be imposed from outside. The benefits of any intervention have to be both tangible and fair. Who does it all benefit most, and who does it degrade? Whose self-interests or purpose does it all serve and what are the trade-offs?

By this time, the discussion and debate unsettles everyone – as it should. Our discomforts derive from having our certainties challenged. It takes time to accept that uncertainty, in particularly the uncertainty of deciding interventions, is not a sign of professional incompetence, as we were taught it was, but rather a condition of practice.

We now explore these discomforts in three ways: in disciplinary work, in interdisciplinary work, and in our search, through narrative or other media, for quality of life – looking to ways of giving expression to one's experience of place.

DISCIPLINARY WORK

We cast our minds back to the woman with the leaking roof, her house, her family, her community, her story. I set a task for the group that enables everyone to explore the value of their own disciplinary expertise in deciding interventions. How would we upgrade or improve conditions? As we brainstorm topics to think about and ideas for intervention, clusters of familiar positions emerge, which serve to reinforce and give value to the expertise we have, although not always the expertise we need. In discussion, there is the usual tendency to define the problem in ways that enable one to exercise that expertise – we shuffle the issues around in ways that enable us to intervene and solve.

Disciplinary stereotypes quickly appear among the group – each discreet in its own right, some more than others. For planners: land tenure, infrastructure planning, land-use planning, housing affordability, reducing densities are all a priority. For the engineers: water, sanitation, safe housing. The social scientists prioritize gender as a theme in its own right and focus on community – what is it and where to find it. The humanitarians target rights and entitlements, children and livelihoods, themes that crop up with others. For the few industrial designers in the group, their exploration in a context that could only be imagined includes transforming bicycle rickshaws into school buses to improve accessibilities; recycling waste into building materials; pumping water more easily and making it fun using seesaws, roundabouts and swings. For all, eliminating poverty, reducing vulnerability, building resilience and ensuring sustainability, recur as themes across all areas of expertise. By which time, for the architects in the group, it seemed that it had all been covered. They struggled more than others to find a role, unable at first to figure out how they could contribute, given all the seemingly more worthy causes. They questioned the value of design. Are architects really necessary?

The discussion among this group started, as if often does, with sorting out the meaning and purpose of architecture in the context of the latest trends in urbanization, the current relevance of new urbanism, the threat to cultural heritage and the threat of blurring regional traditions induced by globalization. We went on to discuss the legitimate boundaries of architecture as we understood them historically, with their focus on the physical and spatial form of place and the making of buildings. How might these boundaries be redrawn in ways that enable one to continue to be rigorous and passionate about architecture, and at the same time, in ways that are relevant to some of the big issues outlined earlier? One group, with its intent to improve housing conditions, did what they knew how to do best. They proposed a clever flat-pack, prefabricated, timber-frame house, factory-made, easy to transport anywhere, simple to erect, easy to adapt. In a conventional way, they had assumed their client to be some private developer who, in partnership with the government housing authority, would provide subsidy and regulate land as a part of their upgrading initiatives. Their market surveys had suggested a number of standard housing types as starter homes, which could be modified over time. The whole would come with a well-illustrated manual for families and collectives to self-build, with examples of how standard components could be combined in a variety of ways to meet individual preferences, and how further components could be ordered should families need to extend.[19]

Their proposal seemed perfectly reasonable and more, very current: the state, the market and civil society groups getting together to solve housing problems – all part of good governance; a corporate social responsibility role for the private sector combined with a good business model that would give access to markets; new housing for families that they would help build, reducing costs and mobilizing labour; slums progressively eradicated; and for the architects making the proposal, they would do what they know how to do best – design houses for a single client body with all the technical and logistic processes to put them up easily, cheaply and quickly.

My critique at the time was similar to that levelled by Echanove and Srivastava, reported in the *New York Times*, at the initiative to design a $300 house, which the designers argued, would 'improve the lives of millions of urban poor around the world.'[20] There would, I said, be little or no participation from families or user experts beyond their labour; the prefabricated house, with its standard plan types was a simplistic response to a complex network of social and economic alliances that characterize informal settlements; that the prefab in its mode of production would undermine the assets, livelihoods and resourcefulness of all the carpenters, informal hardware stores, plumbers, masons, component manufacturers, recycling entrepreneurs who proliferate in informal settlements and who, we have now learned, are integral, not marginal to the wider economy; that the ways in which people who earn around a dollar a day save, invest and adapt their houses, was misunderstood or worse, ignored; and that new construction, given existing densities, would promote 'the clearance and demolition of well-established neighborhoods to make room for it all,'[21] resulting often in eviction and relocation in which the architects would be complicit.

Importantly, the architect's proposal, whatever its merits, was grounded on assumptions about purpose and professional responsibility no longer valid today, given the challenges we face. What we need are new assumptions to guide the way we think, do and organize and that unlock a greater and new kind of resourcefulness with which to tackle some of the big issues more strategically: climate change, the greater social economic and environmental complexities of cities, humanitarian crisis induced by man made or natural disasters, poverty, inequality.

First, the prefab house had relegated participation to self-help, denying therefore the opportunity to mobilize the resourcefulness of others, other than their labour. Participation is the qualitative means of accessing and accumulating assets, tangible and intangible; ensuring strategic value to practical work; engaging community in community-led planning; capturing expert knowledge from those who do not normally have a voice in planning; making partnerships – all of which is central to good governance. Their gesture in this respect was at best benevolent to their users, at worst tokenistic or even manipulative.

Second, the prefab house in its assumptions about means and ends had failed to reconcile a basic truth. You do not solve housing problems by just building houses; in the same way you cannot effectively deal with health by just building hospitals and clinics, or education by building schools. Bad housing is a symptom, not the primary cause of deeper problems – of insecurity, unemployment, social exclusion, inappropriate land tenure, lack of social ownership, poverty – all of which are quickly dismissed as beyond the boundaries of architecture. Or are they? The architects, typically, had turned the complex process of housing into things they could design. People became the objects rather than subjects of design.

Third, the proposal had assumed that what housing is, is more important than what is does.[22] If architecture is to contribute to sustainable human and economic development, then the value of projects and programmes must be measured in their ability to generate income and employment, to inhibit environmental degradation, to improve health and build all kinds of tangible or intangible assets – including the social, political, aspirational, physical and financial – an issue we will return to in our discussion of interdisciplinary work.

In 2011, I chaired the jury to a competition promoted and organized by the Royal Society of Arts (RSA) entitled 'The Resourceful Architect.' The RSA firmly believed 'that learning to design helps people to become more resourceful and self-reliant.'[23] How could architects deploy their skills more resourcefully in these changing times to tackle some of the big issues we face today? How might they maintain, reinforce and expand the relevance of architecture and explore more broadly their resourcefulness?

In writing up my thoughts on the issues that the competition process raised, I concluded that design is resourceful when it liberates the resourcefulness of others; when it invites rather than inhibits the abilities of ordinary people to improvise.

Frank Lloyd Wright, in pursuit of his ideal for individualism, recognized the value of improvisation. He envisioned mass-produced components that were sufficiently flexible to enable everyone to put them together in his own way. 'The house,' he was suggesting, 'should grow as the trees around the man himself grow.' Its shape would be determined by the individual's resources, the needs of his family and his understanding of his own land.[24]

Improvisation follows the principles explored recently by Scott Burnham in his essay *Finding the Truth in Systems: In Praise of Design-Hacking*. In summary:

> *hacking represents reciprocity between the user and the designer. While it complicates authorship and challenges the designer's instinct for control, hacking also breaks down barriers between design and people and yields significant benefits in the process, creates new engagements between the product and consumer, mediates relevance and necessity in design, creates abundance from limited resources.*[25]

In their forward to the recent addition of *Adhocism – the Case for Improvisation,* Charles Jenks and Nathan Silver suggest that adhocism denotes:

> *a principle of action having speed of economy and purpose of utility. Basically, it involves using an available system of dealing with an existing situation in a new way to solve a problem quickly and efficiently. It is a method of creation relying particularly on resources which are already at hand.*[26]

'[It] consists of a general and loose approach to a problem rather than a tight and systematic one.'[27] Richard Sennet calls improvisation the user's art. Jamie Young refers to the 'frugality' of good improvisation.[28]

It becomes clear that design and improvisation are complementary. Designing processes that encourage improvisation become as important as the designing of things. Examples are plenty. David Rockwell's 'Playground in a Box' follows the theories of 'loose parts' espoused by Simon Nicholson: 'In any environment, the amount of learning and creativity possible is directly proportional to the number of loose parts in it.'[29] Rockwell's 'Imagination

Playground' comes in a box easily transportable to anywhere, 'with lots of loose parts for children to create their own play spaces, recognizing that many of the elements with the greatest value to children were inexpensive and portable.'[30] The box contains a bundle of bits – blocks of different sizes, blocks with holes, plugs, chutes, squeaky hinges, arched chutes – for example. It can be added to with found parts – cardboard pipes and the rest. It is 10 feet by 10 feet, weighs some 825 pounds and is made of biodegradable polyethlene foam. The components can be combined to make animals, slides, small enclosures, Star Trek androids, climbing frames and more.

In another detailed example, the 'Litre of Light Project' has devised a sunlight-powered light bulb using discarded two litre plastic bottles. Each is filled with a solution of bleached water and carefully fitted into the roof. It refracts the equivalent of 55 watts of light and costs around $1 to make. It produces light, recycles waste and creates jobs in its making and installation.[31]

INTERDISCIPLINARY WORK

After this first exploration into the core value of our expertise, I set the task differently. I set it in a way that is at once more obscure and yet more focused, exploring this time round the value of interdisciplinary work. It is the start to breaking down barriers and crossing boundaries between disciplines and, later, between levels of organizations, between knowledge and know-how.

I ask everyone in groups to consider what housing, water, sanitation does – not just what it is – to add the development agenda of each sector-specific task. And so for housing – it might be to generate employment, teach skills, give security, build a sense of belonging, improve health, consider the environmental impact on materials and technologies. For water, it is significantly about health, about conservation and the anthropology of water, which often inhibits the adaptation of habits, where old ones are confined culturally. Immediately, we discover and begin to articulate the need and value of interdisciplinary partnerships, in addition to the disciplinary standards and doctrine. We discover the need to work with different levels of organization – local, national, even global – in health, environment, conservation and employment generation and across public and private divides.

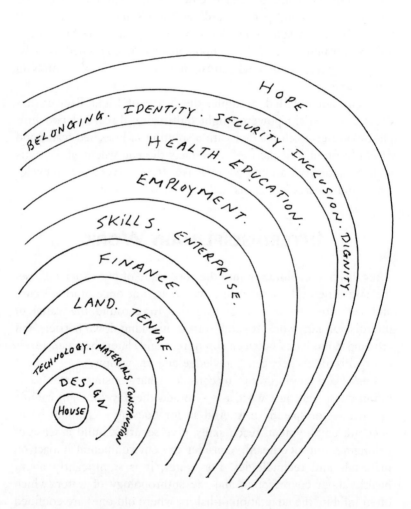

Figure 3.4 *'is' and 'does' – crossing boundaries*

It was Adam Ferguson who wrote in an essay on the history of civil society that:

> *the separation of the professions, while it seems to promise improvement of skill, serves in some measure to break the bonds of society, to substitute mere forms and rules of art in place of ingenuity and to withdraw individuals from the common scene of occupation on which the sentiments of the heart and the mind are most happily employed.*[32]

Two things to think about when it comes to interdisciplinary work. First, interdisciplinary work is not about compromising your professional identity in some middle ground of anonymity and abstraction. Nor is it about consulting others, but more, about redrawing the boundaries of expectation of each discipline in ways that reveal complementarities – as we shall see below. It is about doing what you do best more effectively, tapping the wisdom, expertise and know-how of others, which is the essence of participatory practice.

Second, interdisciplinary work enables you to take advantage of what you do best and to do more with it. It enables one to see what we see from different disciplinary positions and in so doing, ask questions to reveal realms of understanding that may be invisible to any single disciplinary eye and that open up new and creative lines of exploration. If we go back to the distinction made by Turner between 'what is' and 'what does,' we begin to see important relationships between disciplines and between disciplinary work and development. What a house *is*, however you define it, is arguably a disciplinary activity, easily designed by architects, occasionally with the advice of engineers, quantity surveyors and perhaps others. What a house *does* is about livelihoods and asset building, about resilience and development and therefore, inevitably interdisciplinary. Equally, with waste management, what it is is relatively clear; what it can do to raise environmental awareness, generate enterprise, create compost, is about development and invokes a range of activities connecting disparate worlds in sometimes surprising and ingenious ways.

In all these respects, interdisciplinary work opens up lines of communication and builds alliances between disciplines, between kinds of organizations (government, NGOs, youth orchestras, artists, sports teams, local traders), between cultures and between insiders and outsiders, as we shall explore further in Chapter 4.

If you stick doggedly to your own discipline, given the context of work in development practice, you become skilled, competent and even famous, but not always wise or prudent, not at least according to Aristotle (see Chapter 6).

NARRATIVE AND QUALITY OF LIFE

In our third exploration we consider ways of giving expression to one's experience of place, a third layer of understanding based on narrative. We seek to identify themes more so than needs and set criteria for improving 'quality of life.' What would it take, I ask, to make the place in which the woman with the leaking roof lives a 'wonderful place to grow up in?'

In his book, *The Child in the City*, Colin Ward reminds us that for children, the city is both a tactile place and a visual one, full of sensory experience. For children, insecurity translates into a 'lack of social assurance...that the most precious gift that we can give to the young is social space, the necessary space – or privacy – in which to become human beings.'[33] How can we make the city more accessible as a resource, as a learning laboratory, 'whether learning through the city, learning about the city, learning to use the city or to change the city'?[34] How can the community at large take more responsibility for the education of its children? How do we cultivate 'the art and techniques of citizenship, not just through admonitions or through lectures on civics, but from involvement in real issues'?[35] How do we make it all safe, healthy, fun and invoke a mutual collective responsibility for care, full of hope and opportunity?

In all of these qualitative respects, how would we think about water, sanitation, housing, waste management, health, education, if we were to design these services and utilities in ways that cultivate a 'wonderful place to grow up in?'

I get everyone to write their own short narrative based on childhood memories – part real, part fantasy – and then ask for volunteers to tell their story.

The shop under the stairs

Someone recounts the story of the small shop dug into the ground under the public stairway of the block in which they lived. The block had a self-appointed janitor looking after the public halls and stairways who, for a small fee, had informally rented the space under the stairs. The shopkeeper would climb into his dugout every morning and stand waist-high, serving his customers, who would have to kneel to be served. It first had started out as a garment shop. The shopkeeper had discovered, however, the excitement of children, including our storyteller – as they would pass by, stopping as they did at the shop in which the shelves and products, as well as the shopkeeper, was at their height. It was one of the few public places where children and adults could stand and be at the same height.

The shopkeeper had, of course, taken advantage of these frequent gatherings and had begun to sell sweets and school materials. He had provided a few chairs and play equipment outside his shop where children could wait and play or do their homework, and other children were dropped off as, for a small fee, the shopkeeper, with the help of his sister, who lived in an adjoining flat on the ground floor, would keep an eye on them. It didn't take long for the ice cream van nor for the baker's van, a brightly painted three-wheeler selling cake and cookies, to turn up and park just outside the garment shop.

On Saturdays, children would sit in rows outside the shop and wait for the weekly puppet show to start. Sometimes it was straight entertainment. Other times, with the encouragement of parents, it was partially educational – about the trees and vegetables you could grow on rooftops, or how to make toys from rubbish. On other occasions, the children would occupy the shop with their own made products – exercise books made from paper gathered from local bins, cut-out figures made from cardboard. The money collected would pay for basketball hoops or other play equipment.

The shop under the stairs became a thriving business and a resource – a social asset for the community and a financial asset for the shopkeeper and janitor. The public space outside the shop became a social space, in social ownership, mediated by the local public authority. It didn't take much organization to get it all going, incrementally and with the entrepreneurship of the shopkeeper and janitor. Nor did it take long for the shopkeeper's sister to open up her front room on the ground floor as an occasional popup daycare centre for younger children. They had partnered up with the local authority that provided a small fund to buy basic equipment and furniture. It was a vibrant, profitable, safe, informative, friendly place to be – and fun – a wonderful place to grow up in – a far cry from the community centre down the road, gifted by some charity that had lay vacant for years – too far from anywhere, too controlled – which was now occupied by the civil defence.

The shoemaker's stories

I then told my own story of a wonderful place to grow up in. I had lived in Egypt for some years in the Zamalek subdistrict of Cairo before arriving in England in 1951. I would regularly ride on the back of my brother's tricycle – sometimes with friends – exploring freely the streets and neighbourhoods near to where we lived, on our way to playgrounds and sometimes to school. We would regularly stop for refreshment at the shoemaker's shop and listen to stories, which the shoemaker would spin around shoes he was repairing or others he had salvaged from his bins and was recycling for sale. We would be grateful for the stopover – a respite from the hassle and excitement of weaving our way through crowds, passing the man with his pavement tent, an urban chicken farm, the old woman and her pickle jar, pavement barber and his homemade stool, the street cafes with everyone lounging about, smoking their hubble-bubbles, putting the world to rights, and others slapping their backgammon boards with homemade checkers before reaching the shoemaker.

We would sit on the floor and drink Coke or Pepsi, and often join him and his colleagues for lunch. In one of the shoemaker's cabinets were remnants too old to repair but too good to discard, belonging once to people who were famous or infamous. He called it his 'display of important feet.' There were the builder's shoes, the one who was in charge of a building that had collapsed because he had skimped on reinforcement. There were the professor's boots and those of the child who swore she could fly.

Then there was the policeman who was in charge of a busy crossroads where the traffic would come to a standstill for some significant time. I knew it to be a place where hawkers worked. They would work the crossroads selling everything from maps to cleaning detergent, toys and newspapers. For the time they were working the cars, the crossroads would be a safe place to loiter. We would regularly tag behind the younger traders, looking into cars, sometimes helping to carry their wares. The shoemaker would tell how the policeman would stop the traffic for longer than usual, so that all the traders could get to the cars and sell their goods. It was a kind act but also a profitable one. The policeman would receive a cut of the profits at the end of each day for his contribution in stopping the traffic. They had effectively privatized the crossroads into an informal shopping mall. It was unknowingly my first introduction to the informal city, my first taste of 'development.'

The shoemaker would pick up one pair of shoes and describe its journey – from the forests and green fields from where the leather was sourced, to the slaughterhouse and leather factor, its stench of chemicals and animal skins. From China, a faraway place with mountains so high they would reach the clouds, where the shoes were made, their trip across the oceans in boats made of steel and the shops where people would buy. His narratives, I remember, were his version of the cultural history of place, through some of the people he had met, whose shoes he had repaired. They were narratives of shoes and the conditions under which people would work to make them. And then there was his own version of the geography of the world, which he himself could only dream about.

In summary, and in our discussions in class, there were lessons in the importance of permeability, a place with few borders or boundaries it seemed, of fuzzy edges between public and private, play and work, safety and risk, fantasy and reality, streets and shops – all of which had to be constantly negotiated, informative, safe and fun.

These stories and all the other social and learning resources of the everyday are all a part of the social economy and offer social and educational networks of fantastic richness and variety. They reminded us of the school without walls, an experiment first tried in Philadelphia in 1969 and run by its school districts, called the Parkway Education Program.[36] All teaching took place in the community. The search for facilities was considered to be part of the process of education. Art students study art at the art museum, biology students meet at the zoo, business and vocational classes meet on the job, for journalism, for example, at the local newspaper offices, mechanics at the garage. It was the teams working in Cape Flats in Cape Town who also imagined their city as a learning city, where the formal school integrated 'educational spaces such as urban agriculture, playgrounds, cultural activities and sports fields'; 'Imagine,' they wrote, 'an extracurricular system where community leaders and traders provide a range of educational spaces such as cultural centres, media centres, urban farming, bicycle repair shops and sewing workshops where young people develop their talents as well as their business skills.'[37]

What we get is a network of alliances through the participation of a variety of actors, partnerships with a play space organization for schools, the shop traders and other community organizations and enterprises. We build a sense of belonging and therefore of ownership of the city in the city, by children and traders whose contributions are valued; and we get a whole bundle of asset-building opportunities that are tapped in place and cultivated rather than gifted based on all the latent resources that the city offers.

NOTES

1. Jacobs, J. (1994) *The Death and Life of Great American Cities*, Penguin Books, Harmondsworth.
2. Pullen, W. *et al.* (2012) 'Conflict in cities and the state,' Briefing Paper 10, *Urban Conflicts from Local to Global: Why Policy and Practice must Respond at All Levels*, University of Cambridge, www.conflictincities.org
3. Harvey, D. (1990) *The Condition of Postmodernity*, Basil Blackwell, Oxford.
4. Jacobs, J. (1994) *The Death and Life of Great American Cities*, Penguin Books, Harmondsworth.
5. Chambers, R. (1993) *Challenging the Professions*, Intermediate Technology Publications (Practical Action Publishing), Rugby.
6. UNDP (2013) *UNDP Human Development Report 2013. The Rise of the South: Human Progress in a Diverse World*, UNDP, New York.
7. Greig, A. *et al.* (2007) *Challenging Global Inequality*, Palgrave Macmillan, London.
8. International Institute for Environment and Development (IIED) (2011) *Why is Urban Health so Poor even in Many Cities?*, Environment & Urbanisation Brief No. 22, April.
9. Truelove, Y. (2008) 'Protecting displaced slum populations', online at: www.greengrants.org/2008/03/27/protecting-displaced-slum-populations/
10. Chamberlain, G. (2012) 'Families evicted from temple site on India's heritage tourism trail,' *The Observer*, 27 May.
11. Nelson, A. (2012) 'Peruvian dam would imperil way of life,' *The New York Times*, *The Observer*, 27 May.
12. See: Moser, C. (2009) *Ordinary Families, Extraordinary Lives: Assets and Poverty Reduction in Guayaquil, 1978–2004*, Brookings Institution Press, Washington DC.
13. Gensler, H.J. (2011) *Ethics: A Contemporary Introduction*, Routledge, New York, London.
14. UNDP (2011) *UNDP Human Development Report 2011, Sustainability and Equity: A Better Future for All*, UNDP, New York.
15. Gensler, H.J. (2011) *Ethics: A Contemporary Introduction*, Routledge, New York, London.
16. Sen, A. (2009) *The Idea of Justice*, Allen Lane, London.
17. Putnam, H. (2004) *Ethics without Ontology*, Harvard University Press, Cambridge, MA.

18 See: Gensler, H.J. (2011) *Ethics: A Contemporary Introduction*, Routledge, New York, London, Chapter 1.
19 See: Nabeel Hamdi and RSA Design and Society and Architecture Foundation's Call for Ideas (2011) 'Architecture, improvisation and the energy of place', *The Resourceful Architect*, September.
20 Echanove, M. (2011) 'Hands off our houses,' *The New York Times: The Opinion Pages*, 1 June.
21 Echanove, M. (2011) 'Hands off our houses,' *The New York Times: The Opinion Pages*, 1 June.
22 John Turner said 'What matters in housing is what it does for people, rather than what it is.' Turner, J. (1976) *Housing by People: Towards Autonomy in Building Environments*, Marion Boyars, London.
23 See Emily Campbell's Foreword in Nabeel Hamdi and RSA Design and Society and Architecture Foundation's Call for Ideas (2011) 'Architecture, improvisation and the energy of place', *The Resourceful Architect*, September.
24 Fishman, R. (1982) *Urban Utopias in the Twentieth Century: Ebenezer Howard, Frank Lloyd Wright, Le Corbusier*, MIT Press, Cambridge, Massachusetts.
25 Burnham, S. (2009) *Finding the Truth in Systems: In Praise of Design – Hacking*, RSA Design and Society series, London.
26 Jencks, C. and Silver, N. (2013) *Adhocism: The Case for Improvisation*, MIT Press, Cambridge, Massachusetts.
27 Kay, J. (2011) *Obliquity*, Profile Books, London.
28 See: Sennett, R. (2008) *The Craftsman*, Allen Lane, London; and Young, J. (2011) *How to be Ingenious*, RSA projects, London.
29 Quoted in: Ward, C. (1996) *Talking to Architects*, Freedom Press, London.
30 See: Rockwell, D. (2010) 'Unpacking imagination' *The New York Times*, 26 September.
31 See: BBC News Magazine online (2013) 'Alfredo Moser: Bottle light inventor proud to be poor,' reported by Gribby Zobel, 13 August, online at: www.bbc.co.uk/news/magazine-23536914.
32 Ferguson, A. (1996) *An Essay on the History of Civil Society*, Cambridge University Press, New York; quoted in: Sennett, R. (2003) *Respect: The Formation of Character in an Age of Inequity*, Allen Lane, London.
33 Ward, C. (1990) *The Child in the City*, Bedford Square Press, London.
34 Ward, C. (1990) *The Child in the City*, Bedford Square Press, London.
35 Ward, C. (1990) *The Child in the City*, Bedford Square Press, London.

See also: Griffiths, J. (2013) *Kith: The Riddle of the Childscape*, Hamish Hamilton, London. Joanna Kavenna (2013) 'Babes in the woods', *The Literary Review*, May, quotes Griffiths: 'Children have been exiled from their kith, their square mile, a land right of the human spirit. Naturally kindled in green, they need nature, woodlands, mountains, rivers and seas both physically and emotionally, no matter how small a patch; children's spirits can survive on very little, but not on nothing. Yet woodlands are privatized…while even the streets – the commons of the urban child – have been closed off to them.'

36 See: Ward, C. (1990) *The Child in the City*, Bedford Square Press, London, Chapter 16: 'The city as resource.'

37 Palmer, H. *et al.* (2012) *Change Making, Dealmaking, Spacemaking: Notes on Cape Town*, Royal Institute of Art, Stockholm.

4

CROSS-CUTTING THEMES: OWNERSHIP, ORGANIZATION AND ASSET BUILDING

In our final session we consider together what we believe to be themes that cut across all sectors and that build our development ambitions irrespective of our disciplinary or sector specific interests.

I ask everyone to write a mission statement that we then deconstruct. First, the usual litany of universal themes and buzzwords, difficult to contest, 'warmly persuasive'[1] and often difficult to define in specific terms: rights, gender equality, empowerment, resilience, sustainability, good governance, equality and opportunity. Its easy at this point to become cynical, to point out that 'words that once spoke of politics and power have come to be reconfigured in the service of today's one-size-fits-all development recipes, spun into an apoliticised form that everyone can agree with, (evoking) a comforting mutuality, a warm reassuring consensus.'[2]

How then to configure these themes in ways that are place specific and practical? How can we best shape their meaning and subsequently the means of achieving their ambitions according to the realities on the ground? How best to reintroduce politics and power meaningfully in our debate about development without taking to the streets?

First, however, we deconstruct the meanings behind some of these themes, with a short exercise, which I entitle 'Buzzwords in Other Words.' We take one or two examples of mission statements and have their authors make presentations, this time without using the usual buzzwords – development, sustainability, participation, civil society. What we get, as illustrated in Figure 4.1 are two things: first, the alternative meanings we associate with some of the

CROSS-CUTTING THEMES 45

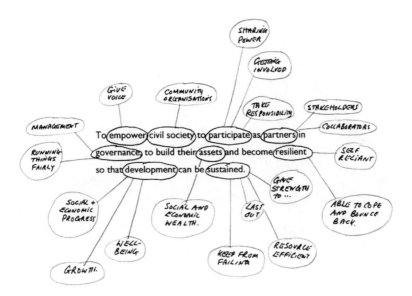

Figure 4.1 *Buzzwords in other words*

words. Poverty reduction for example is about making things less and assumes measurability. Poverty alleviation however is about making things better; second, we consider chains of equivalence where 'the more words that become part of the chain (for example sustainable community development), the more the meaning resides in the connection between them.'[3] In these ways we often invent development models to suit our purpose and reinvent ourselves without, arguably, changing much.

In the diagram below we return to a number of crosscutting themes and look at the ways and means of grounding these in time and place. Figure 4.2 illustrates a model that I have found useful in shaping and evaluating projects and programmes according to their effectiveness in achieving our big purpose.

I define a cross-cutting theme as that which offers the means with which to achieve our big purpose, not the purpose itself. How, for example, do we achieve gender equality, resilience, sustain-

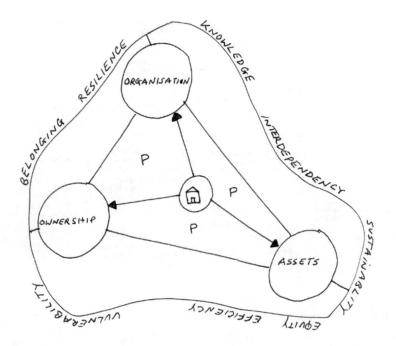

Figure 4.2 *Everything is connected*

ability? I have learnt from projects and programmes from everywhere that three related themes constantly recur as a measure of the success and failure of programmes, a measure of their sustainability and their potential for scaling up: ownership, organization and asset building. All are active processes designed to deliver our big purpose. Ownership comes in various forms. First, ownership of the problem. One hears regularly, albeit after extensive expert surveys and situation analysis, people being told 'your problem is…' Telling people that their problem is bad housing, whatever the root causes and whatever the evidence, when their priority is better education or more employment, is not a good way of engaging either their interest or their participation in any improvements. Our understanding of problems has therefore to be cultivated and worked towards and our priorities negotiated – the key function, often overlooked, in participatory work.

Then there is ownership of the proposal for solving problems, crafting whatever is proposed in ways that fit needs, aspirations and budgets. We need also to consider ownership of assets individually and collectively and at different scales of organization, safeguarding the commons for example on a local and a city-wide level. With ownership – in particular with social ownership – comes a sense of belonging and a commitment to now, soon and later, a commitment to place.

And yet, while we know that place can mediate in building that sense of belonging:

> *it can [also] act as a constraint by limiting people's own ambition for themselves...Attachment to locality based on strong family and social networks in deprived neighbourhoods can limit people's horizons and willingness to consider opportunities elsewhere. However, strong social networks can also foster resilience within deprived neighbourhoods,*[4]

This last point is also true at a city-wide level – an issue to which we will return in Chapter 7.

Second and self evidently, we need organization – to take collective ownership, safeguard the public interest, generate enterprise and scale things up in size and impact. We need place-based organizations – civil society groups networking horizontally with other place-based organizations (for example, the federation of tap attendants) and integrating programmes across a series of vested interest groups (for managing water, setting locally agreed limits to individual excess, growing food, for example) and vertically in partnership with local government institutions. Both place-based and networked organizations need the capacity and the power for independent action – not the capacity to copy.[5] They need the skills, the knowledge and the political space in which to act.

Third, both ownership and organization, also by now self evident, are fundamental to accumulating and retaining assets, individually and collectively – for sustaining livelihoods, reducing vulnerability and building resilience.[6]

If we now place at the centre of the diagram in Figure 4.2 any intervention however detailed – a standpipe, a paved walkway, a community centre, a savings scheme, a health awareness programme, a leaking roof – we can begin to see how success can be engineered and its performance and progress evaluated. Importantly, ownership organization and asset building have to be negotiated in the triangular spaces in between, with the participation of all stakeholders (in the diagram) rather than imposed, all of which makes each place specific in its formulation, and more, gives specific meaning to our big purpose.

Two further observations on Figure 4.2: first, it doesn't matter where you start, but it does matter that all the pieces are connected. As we move inwards from purpose at the periphery toward the centre of the diagram in search of beginnings, so it will be essential to work backwards from inside out, from project to purpose making it all practical. Alternatively, if we suspend our big purpose and start with a more detailed intervention, as we did with our example of the leaking roof, so it will be necessary to build out to the periphery in search of a purpose meaningful to all and then returning to the centre, crafting ownership, building organization and assets. In so doing we expand the opportunities inherent in fixing leaking roofs – take advantage of their development and more strategic potential. These themes and their application we will explore again in Part 3.

The second observation and driving it all, is about participation – my own core theme through which I have learnt to reintroduce politics and power back into the debate on development – crafting partnerships, not so much so that power can change hands but rather so that 'ideas can change minds.' It would be inconceivable to achieve many of the big ambitions for development that we listed at the start of this chapter without the kind of participatory democracy, which offers people hope and the ability to shape worlds in ways that are just. I end our introductory sessions with the diagram in Figure 4.3.

CROSS-CUTTING THEMES 49

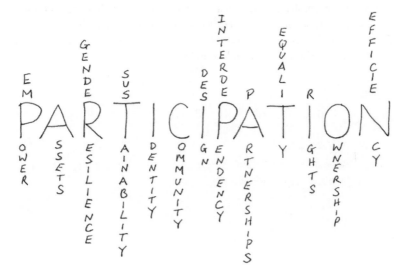

Figure 4.3

NOTES

1 Cornwall, A. and Brock, K. (2005) 'What do buzzwords do for development policy? A critical look at 'participation,' 'empowerment' and 'poverty reduction,' in *Third World Quarterly*, 26 (7).
2 Cornwall, A. and Brock, K. (2005) 'What do buzzwords do for development policy? A critical look at 'participation,' 'empowerment' and 'poverty reduction,' in *Third World Quarterly*, 26 (7).
3 Cornwall, A. and Brock, K. (2005) 'What do buzzwords do for development policy? A critical look at 'participation,' 'empowerment' and 'poverty reduction,' in *Third World Quarterly*, 26 (7).
4 Taylor, M. (July 2008) *Transforming Disadvantaged Places: Effective Strategies for Places and People*, Joseph Rowntree Foundation 'Round-Up,' York. The Arts, in particular theatre, can be an effective catalyst in building a networked rather than place-based sense of belonging.

See for example: 'Hidden theatre offers a sense of belonging,' reported in the Arts section of *The Herald*, Wednesday 27 June 2012.
5   Sennett, R. (2003) *Respect: The Formation of Character in an Age of Inequality*, Allen Lane, London, p176.

PART 1 SUMMARY: THINGS TO THINK ABOUT

> *There is a pervasive dilemma that occurs in research, in planning, and in politics. How much can you afford to know before you act? How much time can you afford to spend making sure that you will all act together? How far can people share power without destroying the power they share?* [1]

It's easy deciding on purpose, given all the issues we confront and our passion to change worlds, to do something big and lasting. Its easy to be worthy, to stick to the high ground, to exercise one's moral authority in deciding the way forward. It's easy to decide what *should* be done, to find answers to generic problems based on the wealth of research and experience and all the casework we bring. It's much more difficult to sort out what *can* be done in the face of all the constraints, to search out significance in seemingly insignificant daily routines, to find meaningful beginnings. It's expedient to scope out comprehensively the problem as one sees it or has seen it before, before we start to find solutions. It's much more difficult, less tidy, less predictable in outcome to 'learn about the structure of a problem in the process of solving it,'[2] to get a good enough sense of its scope to get one going, to move from understanding *before* action to understanding *in* action.

When it comes to deciding how to decide where and how to intervene, we considered five integrally related routines. In 'Ways of seeing – looking and listening', we questioned our values and the way in which they shape our perceptions – about private and public domains, about order or disorder, about the value of informality. We searched for questions of how things work or don't, looking for clues where best one might start, recognizing the need to understand both the visible and invisible structure of place – its resourcefulness, not just its problems.

Second, we considered the ethics of how to decide, the objective view, the value of facts and evidence as a basis for imposing decisions albeit in the public interest – the moral realists versus the relativists, and those in the space in-between, where most answers will be found. Our purpose was to challenge again the value of expert or outsider views, the level of compromise or risk one would be prepared to assimilate in the time it usually takes for the social transformation necessary for change to happen – rather than to be imposed.

Third, there are the values and rationale we bring in disciplinary work, with its tendency to be more sector specific, more practical, more targeted – to housing, water, sanitation, health, education, for example. Fourth, we broadened the scope of this work, redrawing the boundaries of expectations of each discipline in relationship to others, asking not just what housing is, for example but what it can do, taking advantage of what each does best and doing more with it. In so doing we added the longer term more developmental agenda of rights, security, asset accumulation – working back to our big purpose of giving voice, reducing vulnerability, ensuring our projects and programmes are sustainable.

Fifth, we explored the way in which narrative can give expression to our experience of place, can help shape our understanding of the quality of life in place in making it all, for example 'a wonderful place to grow up in.' We looked again at relationships between city places, city functions and city organizations, formal and informal. We did this in order to understand and take advantage of the resources available for learning and for innovation, to build a sense of belonging – a sense of citizenship and respect.

Finally, we brainstormed a number of what we considered to be cross-cutting themes – rights, gender, sustainability, empowerment – all of which I argued are achievable through participatory practices. We considered the three causes of failure or success in sustaining most projects and programmes and of scaling them up – organization, ownership and the ability to accumulate and retain both tangible and intangible assets. We developed a model with which we would evaluate projects and programmes accordingly – in which we start with our practical intervention at the centre, however detailed – a standpipe, a house, a bus stop a leaking roof – which would then, through participation and partnerships, help build organization, ownership and assets. The results, as we have seen everywhere, are a greater resilience, a stronger sense of belonging, more easily sustained programmes and all the other results that contribute to our big purpose.

Notes

1   Stretton, H. (1978) *Urban Planning in Rich and Poor Countries*, Opus, Oxford University Press, Oxford, Melbourne and New York.
2   Kay, J. (2011) *Obliquity*, Profile Books, London.

PART 2:
THE SPACEMAKER'S GUIDE TO BECOMING STRATEGIC

The political problem of mankind is to combine three things: economic efficiency, social justice, and individual liberty.
John Maynard Keynes

5

EQUITY, EFFICIENCY AND PARTICIPATION

It would be easy to be pessimistic about Keynes's ambition, given today's political climate and the rising tide of global inequality. That pessimism is summed up in Leonard Cohen's lyrics to his song, *Everybody Knows*.

On 4 February 2013, I attended a panel discussion at the RSA on 'Placing Sustainability at the Heart of Housing.' I was asked to say a few words on the importance of participation in sustaining housing and urban development. I started with an assumption that I have tested internationally in diverse, and sometimes volatile, cultural, economic and political settings, and that continues to be my cause for optimism. Participatory practice is both efficient and equitable and more, it converges these two worlds in sometimes surprising and creative ways. It does so because with it, you embark upon a process of discovery in which everyone involved has a vested interest. It is fundamental to building community, which I have come to realize is equivalent to building the social economy of place. That is, the local economy of collective assets and networked resources, tangible and intangible, which are necessary for wellbeing, for taking action and for building and sustaining livelihoods. Participation is fundamental to human development. It is fundamental to expanding people's freedoms and capabilities to lead lives that they value and to expanding their choice. This surely, by now, everybody knows.

Participation is efficient because it provides a lens through which to observe and build our collective understanding of the order and disorder of city life. It makes visible the invisible structure of place

– its social networks and alliances, its cultural heritage and the aspirations of its people. It enables us to discover and celebrate our sameness and, at the same time, to respect and accommodate our differences in needs and aspirations, and to articulate these more accurately and more ethically. It enables developmental practitioners to explore more creatively alternative forms of provision and co-production in housing, services and utilities, as well as alternative forms of ownership and management.

Participatory practice is efficient because it is a good way of mobilizing resources that are often latent in community and because over the longer term it reduces dependency (while searching out and respecting it when and where it is needed) and builds resilience – that ability to resist, cope with and recover from the cycle of shocks and stresses common to all, in particular to vulnerable communities.

The evidence of efficiencies is plentyful and convincing. In the UK, the evidence of participatory budgeting is that 'when people are taken through an iterative, well facilitated process of prioritizing their local budget, they vote for the most vulnerable and needy people.'[1] Look, for example, at participatory budgeting in Brazil, where citizens are directly engaged in deciding public expenditure in the community. Look at all the work of the Asian Coalition of Housing Rights (ACHR), of Homeless International, of the People's Dialogue and many others. In the UK, look at the Glass House project – a community-led design process that demonstrates how, when the design process engages local people and civil society organizations, it can save valuable time and resources in project design, management and delivery. Research by the organization Involve shows how participation can improve the efficiency and effectiveness of public spending and services, promoting social cohesion and social justice and improving wellbeing. In the US, the New York-based organization Solidarity, in its report *Growing a Resilient City*,[2] argues the importance of engagement in creating an economy for people and the planet, building 'value chains' that enhance a community's collective wealth. Claire Bishop in her paper, *The Social Turn: Collaboration and its Discontents*,[3] puts it succinctly: 'The creative energy of participatory practices rehumanizes – or at least de-alienates – a society rendered numb and fragmented by the repressive instrumentality of capitalism.' In this sense, inefficiency is fuelled by inequality. Joseph Stiglitz puts it this way:

> *excessive inequality amounts to sand in the gears of capitalism, creating volatility, fueling crisis, undermining productivity and retarding growth...It not only violates moral values, but also interacts with a money-driven political system to grant excessive power to the most affluent...concentrated economic power converts into political power*[4]

It often denies people the opportunity to contribute in anything other than their servitude. This lack of opportunity, says Stiglitz, 'means that society's most valuable asset – its people – is not being truly utilized.' According to Moser,[5] opportunity, empowerment and security are three key components for alleviating poverty. In summary, 'most individuals would rather accept an inefficient outcome of systems rather than an unfair one.'[6]

The UNDP, in its *Human Development Report 2013*, cites four specific areas of focus for sustaining development: enhancing equity; enabling greater voice and participation of citizens, including youth; confronting environmental pressures; and managing demographic change. Its report calls for a critical look at global governance institutions to promote a fair and more equal world. 'Unless people can participate meaningfully in the events and processes that shape their lives, national human development paths will be neither desirable nor sustainable' and it concludes, as does Stiglitz, that 'growth is generally much more effective in reducing poverty in countries where income inequality is low than in countries with high inequality.'[7]

Participatory practices promote greater equality. They promote equity in governance 'the steering and control of society and the economy through collective action.'[8] They are fundamental to renegotiating power relations, for building ownership and the right to live in dignity, to removing discrimination and ensuring that people gain fair access to essential resources (knowledge, materials, land, etc.) to meet their needs, build their assets in order to reduce their vulnerabilities, and build their capability to act.[9] This also everybody knows.

It was Robert Kennedy who said:

the gross national product does not allow for the health of our children, the quality of their education, or the joy of their play. It does not include the beauty of our poetry or the strength of our marriages, the intelligence of our public debate or the integrity of our public officials. It measures neither our wit nor our courage, neither our wisdom nor our learning, neither our compassion nor our devotion to our country; it measures everything, in short, except that which makes life worthwhile.[10]

Definitions of participation today vary in content and emphasis but not often in ambition: 'people engaging with each other for the common good;' 'exercising voice and choice and developing the human, organisational and management capacity to solve problems as they arise in order to sustain the improvements.'[11]

My preferred, if simplified, definition is: taking responsibility with authority in partnership with other stakeholders in the governance of place. That is, 'it demands cooperation more than solidarity, finding ways of holding people together who are very different, who don't understand each other and maybe don't even like each other.'[12] It demands the kind of skills embedded in action science, and it demands practical wisdom – which we will explore in more detail in Part 4.

Difficult, some might say, in an age where 'the pursuit of individual advantage trumps obligations to others, and what society holds in common.'[13] Difficult indeed in times when 'the rise of right-wing individualism and an accompanying celebration of the private and distrust of the public is undermining the diversity and strength of our social institutions.'[14] Difficult again when electoral democracy would seem to stifle the expression of everyday experiences. 'Genuine democracy enables ordinary people to break free from the conventions that limit their the capacity to lead fulfilling lives.'[15]

Among all the other difficulties often expressed about participatory practice (it takes too long, raises expectations, plays into political polarities, exploits minorities, demands a high level of agency coordination, can be coercive), one stands out in respect to our own professional uncertainties. That is, for some, it interrupts creative work and is therefore professionally threatening. People, some say, get in the way of creativity and clutter up the process. The reflective concerns and self-questioning of one artist – Elaine Speight, working in a community in West Bromwich, UK, are insightful in this respect:

> *Surprisingly, it was the many meandering discussions about participation that compelled me to re-evaluate my methods and question my motives. As an artist and curator who works in a non-gallery context, participation is well-trodden ground. I have read books by other artists, curators and critics that evaluate or promote participatory practices, re-classifying them as 'New Genre Public Art,' 'Dialogical,' 'Connective' or 'Relational Aesthetics' and 'Socially Engaged Art.' I have debated the instrumentalisation of participation with New Labour cultural policy, its creeping alignment with the Coalition's Big Society rhetoric and the artistic value of projects that privilege social process over cultural product. And yet, bizarrely, I had never really interrogated my own reasons for involving people in the work I make, or the ways in which I do so.*
>
> *Witnessing the methods and extent of participation engendered by the group's individual practices encouraged me to reflect upon its purpose within my own. What would happen if, like Laurence Payot or David Boultbee, I relinquished the duty of completing the artwork to hundreds of strangers; many, many, more people than I have ever directly involved in any of my own projects and, to be frank, a terrifying prospect? Would such a move better help me achieve my ambitions for the work or simply dilute its quality? Or, more drastically, what if I created work that was deliberately non-participatory? What if, as Theo Price advocates, I abandoned the idea of*

participation altogether and created art that sought to exclude rather than include? Would this undermine the democratic ideals of my practice, if indeed any such ideals exist? Or, as Theo suggests, would it liberate me from my part in the myth that participation equals empowerment, and the convenient fiction that 'we're all in it together'?[16]

Lastly, and in urban development, it is difficult to imagine achieving that universal goal of good governance, that political willingness to promote economic and social equity without partnerships, and you can't do either without participation.

Partnerships include:

an association between two or more persons, groups or organisations who join together to achieve a common goal that neither one alone can achieve...Each member agrees to contribute resources with the understanding that the possession and enjoyment of the benefits will be shared by all. Partners work hard to strengthen each other and to endure conflict and change, because they recognize that their shared goal extends beyond the reach of any one member[17]

And because they recognize their collective moral duty to serve a broader collective good. They offer whatever individual wisdom that is brought to the partnership a 'moral oversight' – a 'moral amplification.'[18]

But good governance, everybody knows, means more than just managing service more efficiently. Good governance in search of commonality creates a kind of commons, where knowledge and experience can be exchanged and risks of opportunity can be shared.[19] Three things to think about with respect to governance: first, how to bring back local government as a key stakeholder in a new and revitalized relationship to both private sector and third sector stakeholders. Second, how do we strengthen civil society groups as partners, not just as consumers of housing, service and utilities – how do we build their capacity to engage effectively in new forms of governance? Third, what new relationships or partnerships can we imagine between both and the private sectors, in search of more efficient and more equitable forms of governance?

NOTES

1. Twivy, P. (2012) 'Why Cameron's Big Society failed', *The Guardian*, 14 November.
2. Solidarity (2013) *Growing a Resilient City*, Solidarity, New York.
3. See: Bishop, C. (2006) *The Social Turn: Collaboration and its Discontents*, Arts Forum, City University of New York (CUNY), New York.
4. Stiglitz, J.E. (2012) *The Price of Inequality*, WW Norton & Company, New York, reviewed by Edsall, T. (2012) 'Separate and unequal', *The New York Times Book Review*, 5 August.
5. Moser, C. (2009) *Ordinary Families, Extraordinary Lives*, The Brookings Institution, Washington DC.
6. Stiglitz, J.E. (2012) *The Price of Inequality*, WW Norton & Company, New York, reviewed by Edsall, T. (2012) 'Separate and unequal', *The New York Times Book Review*, 5 August.
7. UNDP (2013) *Human Development Report 2013. The Rise of the South: Human Progress in a Diverse World*, UNDP, New York.
8. Torting, J. et al. (2012) *Interactive Governance: Advancing the Paradigm*, Oxford University Press, Oxford.
9. Moser, C. (2009) *Ordinary Families, Extraordinary Lives*, The Brookings Institution, Washington DC.
10. Robert Kennedy quoted in *The New Economics Institute Newsletter*, January 2013.
11. Saxena, N.C. (2011) 'What is meant by people's participation,' in Cornwall, A. (ed.) (2011) *The Participation Reader*, Zed Books, London.
12. Sennett, R. (2012) 'Beyond solidarity,' *New Internationalist*, NI 454 July/August.
13. Hutton, W. (2012) 'Born poor? You won last prize in life's lottery,' *The Guardian Weekly*, 20 July.
14. Hutton, W. (2012) 'Born poor? You won last prize in life's lottery,' *The Guardian Weekly*, 20 July.
15. See: David Runciman's 2013 review, 'Something has to give' of David Graeber's book, *The Democracy Project: A History, a Crisis, a Movement*, in *The Guardian Review*, 30 March.

16 Speight, E. (undated) *Palimpset*, part of the Longhouse Action Research Project, West Bromwich, in collaboration with Multi Story, a community arts organization.
17 Poole, D.L. (1995) 'Partnerships buffer and strengthen,' *Health and Social Work* 20(1).
18 Quoted from a lecture by Chris Malone at Wolfson College, Oxford, 25 February 2013.
19 Harvey, D. (2012) *Rebel Cities: From the Right to the City to the Urban Revolution*, Verso, London, New York.

6

EQUITY, EFFICIENCY AND CITY FORM

Efficiency and equity and their convergence are recurring themes now, as in history, in our search for social and economic wellbeing and in our efforts to build the resilience of place. Each wrongly competes for dominance in political and social space. Efficiency today is typically the mandate of market-driven or private sector initiatives; equity is left to the public sector, to charities and NGOs to sort out and to ensure the provision of safety nets to lessen the burden of inequity that results from the progressive privatization of urban place. The physical and spatial form of our cities and their architecture serve to reinforce these divisions.

David Harvey, writing with reference to the forces which shape our cities today – class, power, possessive individualism, the rich elite – says:

> *we increasingly live in divided, fragmented and conflict prone cities…The results of this increasing polarization in the distribution of wealth and power are indelibly etched into the spatial form of our cities, which increasingly become cities of fortified fragments, of gated communities and privatized public space kept under constant surveillance.*[1]

Many commentators on city form echo his analysis – in particular, the impact of excessive privatization of public assets on city life, its character and its social institutions. Arif Hassan, for example, in his study of Asian cities, concludes that poor communities are being evicted from public land to make space for elite private developments. In the drive for foreign investment, the nexus between politicians, bureaucrats and developers has strengthened and therefore zoning regulations and by-laws have become easier to violate in the interests of attracting capital and not improving the wellbeing or life chances of people.[2]

Anna Minton, in her book *Ground Control*, reflects on the way in which planning controls are often negotiated to give the market free reign to turn the city into private enclaves, where security is handed over to private security firms and creativity is

> *carefully scripted by managers of business districts and shopping malls…Street theatre and bunkers are auditioned and their performance timetabled and choreographed to take place in certain designated spots, which means that the unexpected rarely happens … 'we prefer planned creativity,' said one manager. 'We make huge efforts to import vitality.'*[3]

Minton goes on to conclude that 'the consequence of running places like this is that it removes all the imagination and creativity from city life.' And yet, these are the very controls that are considered central to the efficient management and security of place.

Under the guise of making places defensible and managing safety more efficiently, behaviour is being carefully monitored and controlled, play is strictly designated to play areas, public spaces are restricted in use to largely passive activity. Minton's conclusion is that defensible space, 'secured by design,' 'produces isolated, often empty, enclaves which promote fear rather than safety and reassurance.' She goes on to suggest that the best way of changing behaviour is not just by controlling the environment, but also by improving the social conditions that induce fear and crime in the first place.[4] That is, 'being afforded the same rights, dignity and freedoms as other people. These include rights to access resources, the dignity of being seen as able and the freedom to choose to make of your life on an equal footing with others.'[5] It is difficult to imagine how these rights and futures can be secured without the participation of those to whom they are directed.

Charlotte Lamansk, in her research on cities in South Africa, comes to similar conclusions. She reveals the violence that emanates from the inequalities of city life and the progressive gatedness of communities in response to fear, not just fear of crime, but also fear of difference. Gatedness and progressive privatization reinforces inequality. What follows, she suggests, is a withdrawal from public space into private enclaves, making public space unsafe. This retreat from public space promotes more inequality and separation, more exclusion under the guise of more safety.[6]

In the UK, Colin Ward traces the emergence of the privatization of public assets and the erosion of community back to the New Town's movement:

The most telling parable of the privatization of public assets comes from central Milton Keynes…[where] instead of a high street, it has a shopping building at the heart of town…the new towns from Stevenage to Milton Keynes present the same melancholy picture as the old towns described by Ken Woppole: 'The owners of the shopping malls often have no direct interest in retailing and certainly not in the life of the towns they are located in, for the majority of owners are pension funds and insurance companies which have invested in retail property as a part of a wider portfolio…Their interest in the towns where their money is invested in is remote, if not non-existent; it is a financial relationship only, and only questions of the long-term economic viability of town-centre retailing will bring these companies to the local civic table.'[7]

Similar issues were prevalent in the US. The historian David Boorstein, in his critique of the processes of suburbanization in the US, says:

In large developments where the developer had a plan, and even in the smaller developments, there was a new kind of paternalism: not the quasi-feudal paternalism of the company town, nor the paternalism of the utopian ideologue. This new kind of paternalism

> was fostered by the American genius for organization, by the rising twentieth-century American standard of living, and by the American genius for mass production. It was the paternalism of the marketplace. The suburban developer, unlike the small-town booster, seldom intended to live in the community he was building. For him community was a commodity, a product to be sold at a profit. And the suburban homeowner often moved into a whole town which had been shaped in advance by a shrewd developer's sense of the market.[8]

Today private developers and consortia continue to dominate in our cities and towns, particularly in financing and building housing, schools, public spaces, community centres and managing security. Our concern here, however, is less who initiates, but more, with whom and how. Places in the UK, such as Cambourne near Cambridge and Fairford Leys near Aylesbury, are more examples of investment opportunity, overly planned with overly controlled standards from the outside, without much choice or care for community.

John Harris, in his article 'Welcome to Toy Town'[9] quotes the writer Ian Sinclair, who on his visit to Cambourne in 2009, described it as:

> A totally non-organic growth – you swipe a computer screen, and create something, and then insert it on an empty piece of ground. The human aspect follows later, and has to make the best of it.

John Harris goes onto suggest:

> If most of Fairford Leys looks surreally neat and tidy, much of that is due to a 16-page set of development control guidelines. Conservatories must not have aluminium or steel windows, or a pitch 'greater than 20 degrees.' The replacement of external doors is allowed only 'if the original pattern and colour is maintained,' and the same applies to gates and railings. Even electricity and gas meters must conform, with 'colours similar to [the] background wall to minimize obtrusiveness if on the exterior of buildings.'

In these ways, places can be planned, managed and secured without, in the words of one manager, 'getting bogged down in the competing needs of different groups.'[10]

While efficiency and safety have been progressively the mandate of increasing privatization and individualization, so too has the promotion of equality been traditionally the mandate of public sector provision and responsibility. This not so much over concern for the poor, but because everyone has come to realize that inequality is a threat to society as a whole.

What the *London Times* reported in 1846 still holds true today:

> *A town of manufacturers and speculators is apt to leave the poor to shift for themselves, to stew in cellars and garrets, nor are landlords and farmers apt to care much for cottages...something of a central authority is necessary to wrestle with the selfishness of wealth.*[11]

The same concerns are echoed today:

> *If the world allows a majority of the earth's increased population to be stuck in squalid conditions, deprived of basic necessities and cut off from reasonable access to mainstream jobs, what outcome is possible other than a huge loss of potential productivity, at best, and rampant social and political instability and environmental disasters at worst.*[12]

It was, after all, the cholera epidemic in England of 1831 that led to the Cholera Act of 1832, which gave the authorities 'power to enter into any home for the purpose of cleansing, fumigating and white-washing;' largely to protect 'the rights and privileges of the dominant classes in society who were threatened with conditions.'[13] This was the start to major public housing interventions.

In the US, events were largely similar. The appalling living conditions of migrants – some 300,000 people crammed into 3000 tenements in New York that had been constructed quickly and badly by corrupt speculative builders, poorly lit and ventilated – led to the health bill of 1864 and the Health Act of 1866. Epidemics such as smallpox and tuberculosis and riots in 1863 panicked the middle class into reforms that would make cities safe for ordinary people: 'Better housing was needed not only to protect the health of the entire community, but to Americanize the immigrant working class population, to impose upon it the middle class code of manners and morals.'[14] Unless conditions improved, 'the poor would overrun the city as thieves and beggars – endanger public peace and security of property and life – tax the community for support and entail upon it an inheritance of vice and pauperism.'[15] Thus, it was that the Tenement Act of 1867 in New York mobilized the government to improve standards of fire fighting, sanitation and other environmental controls.

Many have concluded that few, if any, public responses to poor housing conditions have been benevolent, neither in history nor today; their purpose has been to prevent disturbance, create jobs and fuel industry and therefore economic growth. Globally we now know that:

> *equity, opportunity and the common welfare are inextricably linked – that the potential of improving incomes, education and environmental standards for even the most troubled groups would, in the long run, provide optimum benefits for rich and poor alike. The implied formula: more equity equals more opportunity of quality of life for all classes*[16]

And, as the historian Tony Judt says: 'inequality is not just morally troubling, it's also inefficient.'

In all cases, and in most cities, the essence of the debate to promote greater equality efficiently centred around standards, standardization and more planning controls, and much less about rights. *Picture Post Magazine* in 1941 featured an article by Maxwell Fry entitled 'The New Britain Must Be Planned.' His vision included:

> *Everybody to live in cheerful, healthy conditions which only proper planning can ensure; an attack on the slums; a bold building plan to civilize our industrial towns; plans for industry, housing, schools, hospitals, transport; a plan to get the best out of town and county.*[17]

Given the complexity and density of urban life, carefully packaged and centrally controlled standards were seen to be essential to maintain efficiencies in design, production and management, reduce costs and ensure equal or similar privileges between rich and poor. Equality and efficiency became associated with sameness. The preface to the Greater London Council's (GLC) 'preferred dwelling plans manual' is revealing in this respect:

> *They [should] avoid the need for detailed planning considerations, save duplication of design work and waste of manpower, serve to speed up and simplify the preparation of scheme estimates, and it means the layout of services and other components can be standardized for each, cutting needless repetition...It should be noted that the plans represent a difficult compromise involving a large number of requirements of a technical, economic, mandatory and policy nature, many of which are in conflict. If a plan is modified, it will seldom satisfy all of these requirements, with the same balance of priorities...A type plan is a standard solution for a dwelling having a particular set of characteristics which distinguish it as a basic type. All type plans are designed to meet the requirements of the housing committee, the DOE [Department of the Environment], statutory controls, and as far as possible, existing codes of practice.*[18]

The GLC's intent is well reflected by Le Corbusier in his book *Towards a New Architecture*: 'standardization is imposed by the law of selection and is an economic and social necessity...We must aim at the fixing of standards in order to face the problem of perfection...Standards are a matter of logic, analysis, and minute study; they are based on a problem which has been well "stated."'[19]

Being equal efficiently, came to mean normalizing differences into standards suitable for everyone in general, but no one in particular. It came to mean:

> *simplification and reiteration...Re-engineering the structure of society, discarding what had come before in favor of a new vision of housing and of cities was to be the trademark of modernism...*

The hope that rational design by an omniscient planner could supersede practical knowledge derived from a process of adaptation and discovery swept across many fields in the course of the 20th century.[20]

The result: a loss of individual identity in the service of the greater good, reflected in the uniformity of our built environment. Variety, where it did exist, was the mandate of architects, reflected in the form, colour and materials of our public housing stock and our public spaces. The problem was accentuated when processes designed at times of crisis became, and still are, the norm.

We now know that neither public nor private, on their own, offer equity that is efficient nor efficiency that is equitable. We have learnt that our search for both lies somewhere in-between. Under inequality, whether through the dominance of either progressive privatization or public control, people lose their individuality. We have learnt that 'there is far more variety when we are more equal; when each constituent party and individual is free to express their needs and aspirations individually' and that 'the great world historical idea, that not only the equality of man but also their differentiation is a moral imperative, becomes the pivotal point for a world view.'[21] Nor should we assume some utopian view of social harmony where equality in particular as it shapes the ethics of participatory practice assumes that everyone has the same ability or skill, that all can contribute in the same way. The way forward in participatory practice 'is to accept this and create a society that celebrates individual abilities, but also sees the provision of needs (for everyone) as its most urgent priority. That is the best, most honest route to social justice.'[22] It is the kind of justice and social harmony derived by 'dancing with difference:'

> *The different worlds of culture are not only antagonistic to one another; they conflict only in so far as they compete for attention and resources…They give society texture, durability and resilience. The desire for a social world of perfect harmony is thus fundamentally misguided.*[23]

One can conclude, once again, that people and societies in Simmel's point of view are not necessarily unequal, just different.

NOTES

1. Harvey, D. (2012) *Rebel Cities: From the Right to the City to the Urban Revolution*, Verso, London, New York.
2. Hasan, A. (2006) 'The changing landscape of Asian cities: The case of Karachi,' *Journal of Research in Architecture and Planning*, 5.
3. Minton, A. (2009) *Ground Control: Fear and Happiness in the Twenty-First-Century City*, Penguin Books, London.
4. Minton, A. (2009) *Ground Control: Fear and Happiness in the Twenty-First-Century City*, Penguin Books, London. In Sri Lanka, I noted on my last visit that the government had combined defense and city planning into one ministry: The Ministry of Defense and Urban Development.
5. Dorling, D. (2012) *The No-Nonsense Guide to Equality*, New Internationalist, Oxford.
6. Lamanski, C. (2004) 'A new apartheid? The spatial implications of fear of crime in Cape Town, South Africa,' *Environment & Urbanization*, 16(2).
7. Ward, C. (1993) *New Town, Home Town: The Lessons of Experience*, Calouste Gulbenkian Foundation, London.
8. MacDonald, D. (1996) *Democratic Architecture: Practical Solutions to Today's Housing Crisis*, Whitney Library of Design, New York.
9. See John Harris' article, 'Welcome to Toytown' in *The Guardian Weekend*, 6 April 2013.
10. Minton, A. (2009) *Ground Control: Fear and Happiness in the Twenty-First-Century City*, Penguin Books, London.
11. Burnett, J. (1978) *A Social History of Housing, 1815–1970*, Methuen, London.
12. Pierce, N. *et al.* (eds) (2008) *Century of the City: No Time to Lose*, The Rockefeller Foundation, New York.
13. Bristow, D. (1981) 'The legal framework, the role of the lawyer,' in N. Hamdi and R. Greenstreet (eds) *Participation in Housing Working Paper 58*, Oxford Polytechnic (Oxford Brookes University), Department of Town Planning, Oxford.

14 Lobove, R. (1962) *The Progressives and the Slums: Tenement House Reform in New York City, 1890–1917*, University of Pittsburgh, Pittsburgh.
15 Lobove, R. (1962) *The Progressives and the Slums: Tenement House Reform in New York City, 1890–1917*, University of Pittsburgh, Pittsburgh.
16 Pierce, N. *et al.* (eds) (2008) *Century of the City: No Time to Lose*, The Rockefeller Foundation, New York.
17 Fry, M. (1941), 'The new Britain must be planned,' *Picture Post*, 4 January, 10(1).
18 Quoted in Hamdi, N. (1991) *Housing Without Houses*, Van Nostrand Reinhold, New York and Practical Action Publishing, Rugby.
19 Quoted in Jencks, C. and Silver, N. (2013) *Adhocism: The Case for Improvisation*, MIT Press, Cambridge, Massachusetts.
20 Kay, J. (2011) *Obliquity*, Profile Books, London.
21 Simmel, G. (1971) *On Individuality and Social Forms*, University of Chicago Press, Chicago.
22 Wright, J. (2010) 'More equal than others,' *Geographical Magazine*, quoted in Dorling, D. (2012) *The No-Nonsense Guide to Equality*, New Internationalist, Oxford.
23 Simmel, G. (1971) *On Individuality and Social Forms*, University of Chicago Press, Chicago.

7

PARTICIPATION IN PRACTICE

What then does all this mean for practice and for the development practitioner? There are three things to think about.

THE LIFE AND ORGANIZATION OF PLACE

First, about the life and organization of place, and the structure of community. We need to drop the unhelpful designations of formal and informal with reference to city forms. Instead, we need to recognize the need for two levels of organizational structure to coexist in community – emergent ones (informal) and designed ones (formal).

Emergent organizations are small, self-organizing, creative, flexible. They are resourceful and often ingenious. That is, they have 'an inclination to work with the resources at hand; a knack for combining these resources in surprising ways; and doing it all in a way which is practical.'[1] In these ways, emergent structures are skilled at improvising. In the language of emergence, '[i]t's better to build a closely interconnected system with simple elements and let the more sophisticated behavior trickle up.'[2] Their order and complexity, in other words, are built piecemeal and emerge incrementally:

> The advantage of this piecemeal method of ordering over totalistic planning is that it allows one to disentangle cause and effect and to learn from mistakes; totalistic planning in seeking to change everything at once, has no relative order against which to measure progressive change.[3]

But cities and human societies also need designed structures – physical, spatial, legal, institutional – with rules, standards, routines and rituals, all of which provide us with continuity and stability – a shared context of meaning and purpose – a shared sense of place. These structures with their tendency to be hierarchical more than horizontal serve to moderate individual excess in the interests of the collective good. It is to these structures, said Isaiah Berlin many years ago, that we give up some of our individual liberties in order to protect the rest. The question, however, throughout history as now, is how much order by design there should be, recognizing that too much order gets in the way of individual freedom and reverts to determinism, as we have seen in our earlier examples? Not enough can lead to chaos, even conflict. This shifting relationship between the order of design and the disorder of improvisation, and the continuous need to craft and constantly adjust the balance between freedom and order, public life and private life, individual autonomy and collective good, between self and other, has concerned architects, planners, economists and many others. Managing the shifting relationship is central in insuring design and planning as the means with which to exercise our collective responsibility but without authoritarian control. It corresponds to the need articulated by Ivan Illich for working within natural scales and limits to achieve what he called a 'convivial' situation. 'Once these limits are recognized,' he says, 'it becomes possible to articulate the triadic relationship between persons, tools and a new collectivity. Such a society in which modern technologies serve politically interrelated individuals rather than managers I will call convivial.'[4]

Emergence and design, improvised structure and planned structure become complementary rather than conflicting in their processes and in their ideals; both are essential to the order and life of place and the livelihoods of people. Together, they reflect the need in society for both social coherence and positive freedoms, for both efficiency and equity. Both engage people in different but complementary ways – the first more practical and immediate, looking for starters to get things going and involving a direct and continuous engagement with the social, economic and physical environment. The second more strategic; engaging with the body politic in search of forms of governance, both efficient and equitable over the longer term.

And both are vital in building and sustaining a sense of belonging, which Robert Dunn describes as 'capital,' as a resource. In the kind of cities described by Harvey, Minton and others, that resource gets lost or is threatened and needs often to be rediscovered, because in cities, our sense of belonging is more plural, more networked. Our allegiances are often shared between communities of place, of culture, of interest, of practice and sometimes of resistance.[5] These often compete for our attention and for resources in any one place. And within each, there also will be disagreement and sometimes conflict in ideals and priorities.

'The freedom to determine our loyalties and priorities between different groups to all of which we may belong is a peculiarly important liberty which we have reason to recognize, value and defend.'[6] The cultivation of choice, therefore, when it comes to identity is one principal responsibility of all urbanists, because the ability to choose and interpret according to one's values, beliefs and aspirations reduces our vulnerability to having our identities coopted by systems, plans, others, to exclusion, to violence.

THE NATURE AND SCOPE OF PRACTICE

Second, we need to revise the assumptions on which we decide our interventions and redefine the purpose and scope of practice. We need to redefine the roles and responsibilities of practitioners.

In my two books, *Small Change* and *The Placemaker's Guide* and elsewhere, I give examples of interventions that served as catalysts to improve the social, economic and physical conditions of poor and vulnerable communities as a part of a larger initiative of urban regeneration.

There was the story of the bus stop placed at the centre of an informal settlement, which over a period of four years became a thriving community centre through a series of progressive interventions (street lights, trees, paving, mobile dental clinic, recycling centre) and improvisations (front rooms of houses that bordered the area were turned into shops and cafes, children gathered under the lights to play and do homework, vendors gathered to sell toys, ice cream, drinks and school materials, others to cut hair). There are similar stories everywhere. I came across one in New York's Chinatown, reported in *The New York Times*:

> *It began in 1998 with a routine act of bureaucracy, a decision by New York City's Department of Transportation to put up a pair of red and white metal signs in the eastern section of Chinatown, on a desolate block in the shadow of the Manhattan Bridge. The signs bore the cryptic message 'Bus Layover Area – 6am – Midnight,' in effect allowed private buses to wait briefly by the curb...Each day, hundreds of people descended on the strip...In just a few years, a vibrant, competitive and largely self-contained economy had materialized around the bus stop.*[7]

Then there was the story of the pickle jar – a visible manifestation of an invisible network of elderly people growing plants and vegetables for sale and for themselves. Our intervention was to bring people together on a disused piece of land adjacent to a nearby school with the intent of socializing their collective resourcefulness and increasing their productivity. In time their activities became integral to the school curriculum, teaching children about plant life and nutrition. Occasional school meals were provided. Other schools in the region saw advantage and replicated the programme until in time, it all became a city-wide programme engaging children in healthy eating, in issues of environmental awareness – all run collectively and by mostly elderly people, earning them small amounts of money and, more importantly, giving them back their dignity and sense of worth.

Then there was the federation of tap attendants, a small group of women and children who, in any case, manage the supply of water from local standpipes. The intervention was to create a social enterprise that involved collecting small monies from people in return for securing the standpipe, ensuring supply and undertaking informal deliveries to those who could not fetch water themselves. Over time, a number of similar social enterprises were set up around the city that were subsequently federated. The federation elected representatives who became members of the city's water authority – part of the governance of water. The practical intervention was clear – improving the water supply. The strategic value became obvious – building a community fund that could invest in other local initiatives, empowering women, creating enterprises and, in all cases, enhancing efficiency and equality.

In another example, and following a community-planning event, the subsequent plan, rather than presented in PowerPoint, was presented on a stretch of wall alongside a small public open space with paint pots and brushes available for people to add and modify. The intent was to provide those who had not attended the planning workshop to contribute their views actively, and at the same time to physically improve and socialize the public space and ensure the event remained part of its history. Over time, the mural was transformed by the additions of a much wider group of participants. It had generated a sense of ownership and belonging, not just of the mural and the space, but also of the proposal itself to regenerate the area.

In Guayaquil, Ecuador, it all started with a few pots of paint. The hill at Santa Ana, a historic site in Guayaquil at the north end of the Malecon, was out of bounds to people and tourists because people felt threatened by the largely poor population who inhabited the settlement, and by its seemingly slum conditions. As an extension to the Malecon 2000 Project, a waterside development, the city offered residents a few pots of paint to paint the façades of their houses as well to improve the walkways, streetlights and street furniture. As the history of the place became evident, people and tourists ventured across the divide to enjoy the view and the history of the place. Soon enough, cafes and small shops occupied the streets; income levels rose; gentrification did occur, but to the benefit of local residents. The place became defensible because its public spaces were accessible, lively and inviting, to the benefit of all – not because it was gated. No police, no fences, no walls, no signs – people locally made sure there was no crime.

In Nepal, we witnessed street theatre – a practical intervention designed to inform children about the dangers of snakes after the annual floods. Its strategic value was to build environmental awareness into schools and to ensure through children that schools became a resource for the community on issues of resilience. The children's classroom in this way extended into the community, where groups would undertake surveys, interview families, conduct risk assessments – all of which fed back into the more traditional classroom work in geography, languages, even math. The result: children and schools were to become civil society partners in the governance of place to mitigate risk and encourage the adaptation of local people and habits to issues of climate change.

And then, of course, there is the example of the woman with the leaking roof and all the advantage that we could mobilize, if only we had the courage to ask, 'what if…?'

What then do all these and other stories have in common? What are the underlying assumptions and characteristics in our response? What methods and processes are involved?

First is that common sense adage: if you want to do something big in scale and impact, you start with something small, and you start where it counts. You start where you can; a catalyst intervention that makes an immediate practical difference, but with significant potential for change – to build a new future, recognizing in E.F. Schumacher's words, that 'to talk about the future is useful only if it leads to action now.' All of the examples above illustrate 'the power of just doing stuff' – building often on what people are already doing and doing more with it.[8]

Second, all of the examples – their design and development – are grounded in action research. We adopted an action planning process, where learning and doing go in parallel, not in sequence – where the first action you take tells you something about the next actions you should take. Lindblom calls it 'the science of muddling through.'[9] He contrasts two modes of decision making: 'the root, rational, comprehensive method was direct and involved a single comprehensive evaluation of all options in the light of defined objectives (the master planner or corporate developer). The oblique approach was characterized by what he called successive limited comparison.' Obliquity according to John Kay 'describes the process of achieving complex objectives indirectly. [It is] a process of experiment and discovery, success and failure and the expansion of knowledge leading to reassessment of our objectives and goals and the actions that result.'[10]

Kay's characteristics of the oblique in decision making coincide well with those of action planning: on intentionality, he says, 'outcomes arise through complex processes whose totality no one fully grasps,' because what we intend may not happen; on information, 'decisions are made after recognizing that only limited knowledge of the world is or can be available;' on adaptation, 'good outcomes are derived through continual adaptation to constantly changing circumstances;' on direction, 'order often emerges spontaneously;' on consistency, a 'consistency is a minor, and possibly dangerous virtue' – the hobgoblin of simple minds; and on process rationality, 'good decisions are not the product of a structured and careful process of calculation; good decisions are the outcome of good judgment.' We will explore this issue in more detail in Part 4.

Odd, I always think, how convention has it that first we know and then we act. And only after we have devised the comprehensive plan are we ready to act:

> *While it seems to make sense to plan everything before you start, mostly you can't: objectives are not clearly enough defined, the nature of the problem keeps shifting, it is too complex, and you lack sufficient information, because you always will…Good decision making is oblique because it is interactive and experimental; it constantly adapts as new information, of many kinds, becomes available. Much of that information comes from the process of decision making itself.*[11]

In action planning, and all the examples above, one acts and by reflection one gets to know – what Don Schon calls 'knowing in action.' We think about doing something while doing it, a not unusual routine in most creative work. In so doing, we recognize that 'the problem and our understanding of it changes as we tackle it.'[12] We give ample opportunity for each decision or action to tell us something about subsequent actions, which may induce a change of mind, a change in direction or even a change of objectives. We want to set objectives and later decide interventions step by step with careful attention to the complexity of existing physical, social and economic conditions, building respect for and understanding of the fragility and resilience of place and for what people do and know how to do best.

Learning to do action planning is like learning to reason with your hands, learning to synchronize what you want to do with what is doable. And you cannot rationalize what is doable until you 'enable the art of practice – the daily rite of discovery that is how learning really happens.'[13] Three ideas are crucial in this respect in particular to build on local capabilities and offer a way of tapping the ingenuity of ordinary people and community organizations: spontaneity, improvisation and incrementalism. *Spontaneity* is vital because most problems and opportunities appear and change in fairly random fashion and need to be dealt with or taken advantage of accordingly. Sometimes problems appear all at once and not according to predictable patterns. One therefore has to be selective, knowing that once one problem has been dealt with, another is likely to appear equally randomly. When you have run out of resources but not out of problems, you improvise – inventing rules, tasks and techniques as you proceed. *Improvisation*, as we have seen, becomes a means of devising solutions to solve problems, a process full of inventive surprises that characterizes the informal way in which many poor people gain employment, make money and build houses. The third idea is *incrementalism*. Most settlements grow, consolidate, change and even disappear in a series of increments. Small businesses grow in a similar way, as do houses and communities. The question is to what extent these changes are inhibited or supported. And having answered that question, what kinds of interventions are appropriate at the various development stages?

Third and consequentially, in all our examples, we reversed the usual 'survey, analyse, plan, then implement' routine. Unlocking the resourcefulness of place demands we challenge this linear or 'direct' model of efficiency. Instead, we work backwards. First, and with stakeholders, we profile the problems, opportunities and aspirations. Then we decide on our goals and sort out our priorities. We do our stakeholder analysis, again involving the stakeholders, sometimes in mixed groups, sometimes in separate groups (interest groups, women, children, governmental officials, etc.). Who are the primary, secondary and external stakeholders? What interests do they have in the project, how are each likely to impact it – positively or negatively? What are their relative priorities? Where are our compatibilities and incompatibilities in goals and behaviour? Then together we work out our options for meeting our goals and identify the trade-offs in time, money, capabilities or institutional capacity or political acceptability. We look at some of the constraints likely to get in our way in achieving our goals, who and what – institutionally, environmentally, culturally, politically, financially, technically. And then we decide how to get it all going – a catalyst, which may be expedient in view of all the constraints. We avoid, in other words, pontificating the larger order of things, the big purpose, the policy environment, which may take years to sort out. That first step is monitored and progressively analysed in terms of the next steps it invokes, with all the financial and other implications, from which a larger plan emerges. Any subsequent surveys will be designed to build a better understanding of the primary causes of some of the problems and issues we encounter, because we know that we want not only to deal with symptoms, but with root causes as well. On this basis, more strategic interventions can be decided, ones that tackle the primary causes (discrimination, exclusion, insecurity, poverty) and serve to scale up our programmes. In these ways, both practical and strategic work run in parallel – policy and practice feed each other.

This 'reverse' planning cycle is not a call to get governments off the hook. Nor for removing planning controls in order to give the market free reign to turn the city into private enclaves. Rather, it follows a call from the authors of 'Non Plan' and 'Urban Catalyst' and those promoting 'Unplanned Urbanism' – 'to think of planning as a process that occurs over time and to think not only in terms of desired end results, but rather development steps…which might unfold in several directions where the end result is never defined.'[14]

The coherence of the plan, in other words, is improvised and emerges incrementally in response to problems, opportunities and sometimes competing aspirations. Its rationale and order are induced partly by design and partly by the progressive and seemingly ad hoc spontaneity of decisions in response to needs and priorities, which typically appear and change in a fairly random fashion and often not according to predictable patterns. Our task throughout is to 'navigate successfully through [sometimes] unreconciliable uncertainties.'[15]

In all these phases of work, people participate in workshop settings to decide needs, aspirations, design programmes, following the well-tried routine of action planning. They also participate in direct dialogue with both the physical and social environment that emerges. They hack into and build onto the first interventions, which serve as an invitation to improvise.

Fourth, in all our examples, we were to discover the importance of questioning the way questions are asked, often in reverse order to what first would seem reasonable or rational. In so doing, we were to discover the art of reasoning backwards. We reasoned somewhere in between trickle up and trickle down.

At first, and overall, as we saw earlier in our discussions about the woman with the leaking roof, one suspends one's big purpose, driven as it might be by the pragmatics of meeting deadlines or pursuing one set of political or social ideals versus another, or in pursuit of careers. We avoid asking: what is the most we can do and how can we get it all done quickly and cost effectively? What policy should we change or invent to generate good practice and to make possible our big vision? How can we 'provide' enough housing at affordable costs to satisfy demand? However worthy, whatever our good intentions, these are the kinds of questions that give us our housing estates, master plans and new towns. And 'when good or worthy intentions are tangled with feelings of moral superiority by providers, it can be twice as dangerous. This mixture can encourage "recipients" to feel worthless and third rate; seeing us as "good" and himself as "bad."'[16] The result: a false sense of quality in the exactness of plans and a bureaucratic dreamland of place and community. Worse still, a false sense of achievement among experts, a false sense of excellence. This 'relentless pursuit of excellence is the expert's badge of distinction' and the trademark of top-down providing. It is how we build our reputations and earn our status professionally. It is, however, an antisocial and self-deluding kind of expertise, because it breeds a false sense of self and also another kind of inequality, this time between experts and non-experts. It alienates ordinary people and makes them feel stupid.

Instead, in the examples above, we asked: what is the least we need to do to get things started, or shift what has already been started in more efficient or more equitable ways? And then, what is the most we can do to keep it going and scale it all up in impact? How can our programme and all the intelligence of informality, embedded as they are in everyday practices, inform policy? What further interventions might be needed to generate policies that enable these practices to become more widely accessible in relation to context, to control or modify others that have become malignant or divisive? We now know that good policy derives from good practice and is more connected and therefore effective when it maximizes 'discretion at the point where the problem is most immediate.'[17]

In the examples above, we saw how this could begin to work. With our water tap attendants, partnerships emerged and new policies trickled up for larger scale implementation. What emerged was an alternative form of governance in the supply and management of water. With our street theatre, new policies emerged in education, for integrating climate change into the school curriculum and for establishing schools as knowledge centres for the community at large. In the case of our bus stop, our question, once discovered, was not how do we build a community centre, with all the simplified certainties of what that would involve but rather: how do we cultivate community and let the benefits trickle up, trickle down and trickle across? This led to a series of progressive interventions over time, step by step in place of the one-off 'centre' first envisaged.

Fifth, in our examples and throughout, we see the importance of our first practical intervention becoming increasingly more strategic. Adding strategic value is key to the art of spacemaking and demands at least the following considerations: first, being cognizant of the change it demands and the change that is induced. Change in professional conduct and what it takes to succeed as an expert, which has typically entailed single-solution thinking – to be original, to defend your ground, to be rigorous, to be in control. We need change in practice procedure – in particular, adopting methods and processes that are more inclusive, more participatory and mindsets that recognize that not only are experts special kinds of people, but also that everyone, in their own way, is a special kind of expert. Then there is the change we induce when we intervene, converging the worlds of policy and practice, disturbing the existing order of things when necessary in the interests of both greater efficiency and greater equality. Lastly there is change that we invite and that is integral to practice – that process of progressive improvisation to ensure good fit over time between people, place and the environment.

Being strategic also involves dealing with the primary causes of problems, not just their symptoms. Bad housing is a symptom of failed policies, of social exclusion, of insecurity, of lack of employment. Fixing houses and dealing with the symptoms is relatively easy. Fixing houses in ways in which engage the primary causes invokes the kind of practice discussed earlier (partnerships, participatory practices, enabling policies) as well as crossing boundaries between disciplines, between levels of organization, between knowledge and know-how, as elaborated in Chapter 3.

Schumacher goes further and argues that the ever-increasing proficiency in dealing with symptoms perpetrates the 'violence' that induces bad housing, environmental degradation and poverty in the first place. 'The more skilled we are at dealing with symptoms, the more prepared we are to accept the primary cause of the symptoms as a condition of prosperity.'[18] Schumacher gives us an example:

A very clever chap once said that if an ancestor of long ago would visit us today, what would he become astonished at: the skill of our dentists or the rottenness of our teeth? This is a very neat way of putting it; it shows we cannot reject, we have to be grateful for the skill of our dentists, because of the rottenness of our teeth. This is a mutual escalation: our teeth are still more rotten, and we are still more grateful for the dentists. A nonviolent approach to it would put the best of human intelligence into resolving the question: Why are our teeth rotten?[19]

Across all sectors and disciplines, a number of strategic or primary issues recur and will need consideration in project design, implementation and management: ensuring *ownership*, both of problems and of any new programmes; reducing *dependency thinking*, where problems and their causes are perceived to be other people's responsibility; *lack of knowledge* or information on how to be engaged, how to manage, what implications, risks and opportunities can be expected given any one intervention versus another; *misdirected priorities*, where one stakeholder's priorities dominate all others and where stakeholder analysis is either not done or is incomplete; and the lack of *organisational capacity* is a recurring primary cause, either at the local level, municipal level or both. Underpinning most symptoms are the underlying issues of poverty, of vulnerability, of instability and the inability to accumulate assets, induced often by politics and political rivalry, by conflict and authoritarianism and often reflected in top-down planning that, as with social vulnerability, may result in displacement, repression, exclusion and other forms of discrimination.

Being strategic in practice also demands managing constraints effectively. There are always constraints that are context for work and that may need to be dealt with over the longer term, and constraints that are a barrier to initial interventions. Analysing and dealing with constraints can often lead to innovations such as the federation of tap attendants. It gets one to think outside the box in search of starting points. It often entails converging stakeholder priorities that get in the way of getting going, mobilizing local resources in creative and ingenious ways, imagining new ways of using materials, inventing appropriate technologies, mobilizing unlikely partners. In these ways, constraints both confine and liberate.

Being strategic means scaling up ideas, methods and technologies – not just in size, but also in impact. It means paying attention to our three cross-cutting themes discussed in Chapter 4 – ownership, organization and asset building. And it means constant learning, where the loop of what went well and what didn't and why, what did we learn and, importantly, what difference will it make the next time in the way we think, do and organize is progressively closed. Change of these kinds, derived from lessons learned, is often denied professionally and institutionally because having built up our reputation on doing things the way we now do, we tend to reshuffle the problem to fit the solution we already have devised so that we can carry on as before. As I have said previously, most monitoring and evaluation I have seen is less about learning and more about bookkeeping.

The Roles and Responsibilities of Practitioners

All of which challenges the roles and responsibilities we assume and that are still today promoted in education, whatever our disciplinary core. In my book *The Placemaker's Guide*, I suggest that if we are to link effectively both practical and strategic work and in ways that meet the objectives I have set out, if we are to make space for social and economic development, whatever our disciplinary core, then we have to cultivate four overlapping sets of activity and responsibilities, which I call 'PEAS' – providing, enabling, adapting and sustaining. In summary, to be a good enabler, one has to be a prudent provider, of money, skills, ideas, land, technologies and policies, depending on the programme at hand. Providing on its own, we have learnt, in particular when delivered by experts and often 'outsiders,' is either charity, or reverts to procedures and solutions that become over-standardized in search of averages and lowest common denominators. It induces dependency. Creativity becomes the mandate of the elite and gifted; power relations are reinforced. In any case, providing on its own is unsustainable when reliant on either charities or government, and often inequitable when reliant on private sector initiatives. The value, therefore, of what is provided and how much is partly measured in the practical way it meets the needs of now and, significantly, in the way in which it enables others to provide for themselves, to build assets and become resilient – now, soon and later.

Enabling assumes a number of forms. I take enablement to mean the ability or willingness to provide the means with which to open doors and create opportunities in order to build livelihoods, reduce vulnerability and sustain development – that is, to promote and sustain improvements in the quality of life, particularly to the poor and vulnerable.[20] With *community enablement*, the focus is clearly on people and on building their capacity to be recognized as a key resource rather than a social and economic liability. *Political enablement* is the strategic task of all development practice – to influence policy, change standards, remove discrimination and promote rights. And *market enablement*, opening up markets for small-scale social and other enterprises in terms of skill, produce and products, is a key part of sustaining community. It is integral to our search for good governance. All of which realigns the state and the formal market in partnership with civil society to build and sustain the social economy.

Then there is *design enablement* – thinking about design, whether about housing, education or settlement upgrading as a process of enablement. That is, cultivating an environment of choice and opportunity, encouraging improvisation in search of order – the kind that liberates the resourcefulness of others rather than confines it to second rate. Design as a process of enablement mediates power relations because it leaves opportunity to explore new relationships between things, between people and different levels of organization, between things and people and between all and the environment.

Which leads us to the third component of PEAS – adaptability and change. How should we think about change and resilience as integral to planning and design, knowing that change is fundamental to ensuring good fit over time? It is fundamental to making places convivial, enabling people to stamp their own identity on place, to cultivate over time that sense of belonging. Once again, one needs to revisit what one has provided – too little, too much – and how it enables change.

Finally, in PEAS, there is the issue of sustainability – how do we keep it all going and to scale. Here, it is important to refer back to Figure 4.2 in Chapter 4 to consider again organization, ownership and asset building. Sustaining the social and economic environment of place demands capacities and logistics. It demands organization. Importantly, it demands ensuring ownership and the ability to accumulate assets in order to reduce vulnerabilities. It demands all the demands of enablement – providing catalysts in whatever form, enabling the capacity for change, defining a culture of practice both practical in its objectives and strategic in its purpose, gives us a definition of sustainability guided by an agenda that is practical, moral and meaningful.

NOTES

1. Young, J. (2011) *How to be Ingenious*, RSA projects, London.
2. Johnson, S. (2001) *Emergence: The Connected lives of Ants, Brains, Cities and Software*, Allen Lane, The Penguin Press, London.
3. Jencks, C. and Silver, N. (2013) *Adhocism: The Case for Improvisation*, MIT Press, Cambridge, Massachusetts.
4. Illich, I. (1973) *Tools for Conviviality*, Calder & Boyars, London.
5. For more discussion on the different kinds of community and their interdependencies, see Chapter 11 in: Hamdi, N. (2004) *Small Change*, Earthscan, London.
6. Sen, A. (2006) *Identity and Violence: The Illusion of Destiny*, Allen Lane, London.
7. Reported by Saki Knafo: 'Dreams and discord in vibrant Chinatown,' *The New York Times – The Observer*, Sunday 6 July 2008.
8. See: 'From small beginnings,' reported by John-Paul Flintoff in *The Guardian*, Saturday 15 June 2013.

9   Lindblom, C. (1959) 'The science of "muddling through,"' *Public Administration Review*, 19(2), cited in Kay, J. (2011) *Obliquity*, Profile Books, London.
10 Kay, J. (2011) *Obliquity*, Profile Books, London.
11 Kay, J. (2011) *Obliquity*, Profile Books, London.
12 Kay, J. (2011) *Obliquity*, Profile Books, London.
13 See: Jeremy Denk's article, 'Every good boy does fine': 'you don't teach piano playing at lessons; you teach how to practice – the daily rite of discovery that is how learning really happens,' *The New Yorker*, 8 April 2013.
14 Minton, A. (2009) *Ground Control: Fear and Happiness in the Twenty-First-Century City*, Penguin Books, London.
15 Kay, J. (2011) *Obliquity*, Profile Books, London.
16 Brandon, D. (1976) *Zen in the Art of Helping*, Routledge & Kegan Paul, London.
17 Elmore, R. (1979) 'Backward mapping: Implementation research and policy decisions,' *Political Science Quarterly*, 94(4).
18 Schumacher, E.F. (1980) *Good Work*, Abacus, London.
19 Schumacher, E.F. (1980) *Good Work*, Abacus, London.
20 Fainstein, S. 'Globalisation, local politics and planning for sustainability,' in Haas, T. (ed.) (2012) *Sustainable Urbanism and Beyond: Rethinking Cities for the Future*, Rizzoli, New York.

PART 2 SUMMARY: THINGS TO THINK ABOUT

*The law locks up the man or woman
Who steals the goose from off the common
But leaves the greater felon loose
Who steals the common from the goose.*

Anon[1]

In Part 2, Chapters 5 and 6, we gave context to participation in practice and what it takes to be both practical and strategic when deciding interventions. We began by arguing the importance of participatory practice, giving definition to what it means to generate greater efficiency and equity in development planning. We argued its value in building the social economy of place – that local economy of collective assets and networked resources so fundamental in building community. Participation, I suggested, is the lens through which we build our collective understanding of city life and offers us the means with which to mobilize resources, reduce dependency and build resilience. Its processes, it has been confirmed, are fundamental to human development. They are fundamental to crafting meaningful partnerships and are of essence to good governance.

We went on in Chapter 6 to profile some of the issues that divide and fragment cities today. We saw how these divisions polarize the distribution of wealth, privatize progressively public space and destroy the commons, give markets free reign over urban development and generate gatedness. The result has been to reinforce inequality and to render some cities prone to conflict and violence. We noted in history, as now, how greater equality translates typically into more public control and improved standards for all – how equality came to mean sameness. Greater efficiency came to mean more standardization and more privatization. Both processes are significantly top down in control, and in both, people tend to lose their individual and collective identities. 'More equity,' we noted, 'equals more opportunity and quality of life for all.'

In Chapter 7 we reflected what all this means for practice. First, we profiled the life and organization of place, arguing again for the need for two levels of organizational structure to coexist – *emergent* (creative, spontaneous, improvised, trickle up in impact) and *designed* (spatial, physical, cultural, institutional, legal and trickle down in impact). How much design and how much emergence is intrinsically a function of context and needs to be constantly negotiated.

Second, in the nature and scope of practice, we argued for the need to revise the assumptions on which we decide interventions and redefine the scope and purpose of practice. I suggested that this might entail at least the following:

- To do something big you start with something small and you start where it counts.
- It follows that thinking and doing are parallel rather than sequential processes – where each step you take tells something about the next step, building knowledge in action, 'enobling the art of practice, that daily rite of discovery that is how learning really happens.'
- It also follows that we reverse the order of survey, analyse, plan and implement. We work backwards to move forwards more effectively, navigating our way through all the constraints and uncertainties rather than sorting it all out before we start.
- We questioned the way questions are asked and often in reverse order to what may at first seem rational or worthy.
- Finally was the need to ensure that our first practical step assumes strategic value as well, which entails: inducing change, dealing with the primary causes of problems not just their

symptoms, managing constraints, scaling up in size and impact – methods, ideas, organizations.

Third, we reviewed again the implications of this way of thinking and working on the roles and responsibilities of practitioners, suggesting at least four overlapping sets of responsibility and corresponding criteria with which to structure decisions. In any response, what and how much should we *provide* (P); how this will *enable* (E) people and organizations to provide for themselves, measured in design, capacity and opportunity, at least; how what we provide can be *adapted* (A) over time to ensure a good fit between needs, aspirations, resources and place; and finally assessing again P, E and A in so far as how it can all be *sustained* (S).

Note

1   Anon (1996) 'The common and the goose,' in Jones, M. (ed.) (1996) *Visible Voices*, Channel Four Learning Limited, London.

PART 3:
COUNTRY FILES

The first principle of aid is respect.
                                    Ernesto Sirog

Introduction

While many of the examples illustrated in Part 2 and elsewhere so far start on the ground – mobilizing public interest; spotting small change opportunities of strategic value; tapping into and sometimes modifying local initiatives; federating small organizations into collectives – so the conditions for these initiatives to trickle up and scale up in size and impact are cultivated at the very top. They are cultivated among high-profile actors, often with the UN and other international development agencies, with captains of industry, bankers, housing managers, mayors, ministers and prime ministers. They constitute a client body whose trust and consensus has to be won and whose status has to be respected, even enhanced. We start with sometimes-competing vested interests and often high ideals. Power holders and ambitious politicians, after all, are not that interested in bus stops, pickle jars or leaking roofs – not at first, that is. We cultivate the top by demonstrating how their work will be made easier, their projects and programmes made cheaper and their political ambitions better served by adopting the kinds of practices illustrated so far.

One avoids arguing that their methods and processes are wrong, nor that their procedures are inefficient or their ambitions misdirected or unjust. One avoids challenging their positions, but rather one works with their interests, which we respect and often share, whatever their motives. One avoids, in other words, pointing the finger of blame, but rather, pointing to the way forward. In this way, one does not accept their position as given, but rather, one recognizes their right to that position and subsequently demonstrates through a series of 'yes and...' transformations, how any one position or set of vested interests, albeit modified, can serve the public interest as well.

In his book, *Activism, Advocacy and Democracy*, Aidan Ricketts gives us a common sense working definition of what is meant by public interest:

> An issue that often leads to confusion is the question of whether the public has to agree with you for your cause to be described as a 'public interest concern,' and the short answer is 'no it does not'...In describing yourself or another person as an advocate of the public interest you are not asserting that everyone or even the majority agrees with that cause, but imply that the cause being advocated is a public rather than purely private concern.[1]

It is in everyone's private interests, for example, to cook on open fires, but it is clearly not in the public interest, neither locally nor globally. Ricketts goes on to suggest 'that is not to say that the two never overlap, frequently one person's private concerns also have significant public interest content.' The woman with the leaking roof, for example, was expressing a private concern but with significant public interest potential, albeit to be discovered and explored collectively. The private company advertising its wares on a mast in Lima, which served also as a standpipe delivering drinking water in poor neighbourhood, is another example.[2]

Ricketts goes on to list what it might involve to achieve public interest goals: mobilizing and influencing public opinion, which is equal to building a public consensus about the need for change; tapping into or even modifying attitudes or behaviour; advocating group action to support the cause being promoted; anticipating, considering and possibly countering opposing reactions; strategically engaging with power holders and converging their vested interests in ways that engage public interest concern.

These are the kind of activities that enable urban programmes to be rewritten, with equitable and efficient agendas, according to the principles of participation set out in Chapter 2. It demands we negotiate enough political space that we can occupy with ideas and processes that would structurally change the way we think, do and organize. It all demands the kinds of skills and competencies not easily taught in school – entrepreneurship, flexibility, negotiation, informed intuition, empathy. In all, it demands the acquisition of practical wisdom, which we shall return to in Chapter 4.

My own experience suggests we work in both directions, from public interest to private interest and vice versa, and from top down to bottom up. With the Primary Systems Support Housing and Assembly Kits (PSSHAK)[3] housing project in London, for example, in our early discussions with the GLC and in our presentation to the minister of housing at the time, we started with leveraging greater efficiencies in the design and delivery of social housing – with the argument that participation with council tenants and the ability to adapt dwellings would serve to meet local government targets for housing more effectively; that easily adaptable buildings would ensure a better fit over time between waiting list requirements and the housing stock and would be cheaper to change because the opportunity for change was already designed into the process from the start; that flexibility in deciding the mix of dwelling types and sizes would meet the demands of waiting lists more accurately, saving time and money; that flexibility of interior layouts would meet the needs of individual families more accurately, shortening the time on waiting lists and reducing displacement to other housing estates when needs changed; that mixed communities of families of different sizes, needs and aspirations were healthier and place less burden on local authority to manage; and that the building process itself would be faster and therefore cheaper, taking advantage of both standardization and variety by building shells that could be kitted out separately and flexibly. In all these respects, the participation of families served as a practical need to rationalize the design and construction process and ensure a better fit between home and family, housing needs and local government programmes, place and community. And more, it was all a part of a social movement working at the time toward democratizing housing and the built environment that included a variety of programmes such as Black Road in Macclesfield, Project Assist in Glasgow, Byker Wall in Newcastle, as well as the work of Walter Segal and others. All served to cultivate a social and political environment in which change could happen.

Notes

1 Ricketts, A. (2012) *The Activists's Handbook: A Step-by-Step Guide to Participatory Democracy*, Zed Books, London.
2 See: Prados, A. (2013) 'Advert turns air into drinking water,' BBC News, Science & Environment, www.bbc.co.uk/news/science-enviornment-21899227.
3 For an outline of the PSSHAK Projects, see Hamdi, N (1991) *Housing Without Houses*, Van Nostrand Reinhold, New York.

8

CULTIVATING THE TOP: THE MILLION HOUSES PROGRAMME OF SRI LANKA

In Sri Lanka, the government's public housing programmes, like many in developing countries, were unable to mobilize the kind of money and resources needed, nor sustain the government's pledge in 1982 to provide a million houses. A new paradigm was needed that would be politically expedient and innovative. It would be grounded on participatory practices and on shifting the role of public authorities from providers to enablers, facilitating families and communities to provide for themselves.

These themes were introduced and debated in April 1982 at one of our Special Interest Group in Urban Settlement (SIGUS) seminars at the Massachusetts Institute of Technology (MIT), entitled 'Users and Institutions.' The blurb on the poster read:

> *It is generally agreed that conventional housing approaches and attitudes are ineffective, and moreover, have hindered progress and compounded the waste of human and material resources. In response, an alternative attitude has arisen that focuses on the role of users in management, design and construction, and in so doing, has redrawn the relative role of user and institution in the housing field.*

The seminar went on to review what the new role would mean – its potential, social impact and what practitioners and housing managers need to know for it all to work. It reviewed the economic implications of investment, subsidy and cost recovery, the impact on policy and on housing standards, on land acquisition and the physical alternatives of levels of provisions (core housing, serviced site, roof loan, shell housing, etc.). Participants at the seminar were introduced to these new alternatives – their rationale, methods and aspirations by some of those who had first put the ideas forward – John Turner, Otto Koenigsburger, Horatio Caminos, John Habraken, Lisa Peattie, among others.

For the Sri Lankan delegation, facilitating families and communities to provide for themselves was a timely and more pragmatic means of mobilizing local resources, and fitted well with their new political ideology of 'people's reawakening.' In any case, it was easier to count the house improved and cheaper to provide a core house or serviced site, which can be completed incrementally. At the same time, you could still build a few 'finished' houses for those that couldn't build for themselves, to demonstrate what could be done through community mobilization and enterprise, and to provide the all-important ribbon-cutting photo opportunity.

Sri Lanka at that time was notable for its high literacy rate, a low child mortality rate and a zero rate of urbanization. It had a well-established and well-developed welfare system that reached out into the smallest villages. Sweeping land reforms initiated between 1972 and 1976 enabled nearly 1 million acres to be placed in public ownership, which later gave the National Housing Development Authority (NHDA) substantial flexibility and control over development. In addition, the ceiling on the housing property law of 1973 transferred some 12,347 properties, or 71.6 per cent of all tenements to state ownership.[1]

Immediately prior to 1982, Sri Lanka was very much a provider in housing developments. Its 100,000 Housing Programme (to deliver 100,000 houses to the villages) launched in 1978, and which was to consume some 12 per cent of total public sector investment from 1979 to 1983, did include a substantial amount of direct construction (36,000 units), albeit with a large share of aided self-help (50,000 units). The NHDA was set up in 1979 to deliver lots of subsidized houses and to coordinate the national effort. Policies shifted considerably with the election in 1982, however, partly due to the pressure of party politics (the pledge of 1 million houses that the new government had made with only 3–4 per cent to be allocated out of gross public expenditures would be difficult to achieve without a new paradigm) and partly due to the influence of international trends (notably influential funders and prestigious universities), but mostly due to a number of influential Sri Lankans who saw it as both correct and expedient to shift substantially to support policies. These same people saw an opportunity to gain international visibility from their programme and to endorse their national status in a wider intellectual and political community – all legitimate aims. A small country willing to experiment needs the cushion of international respect, and it needs to have its successes and mistakes, if and when they occur, legitimized in the interests of learning.

In 1984, the NHDA's 'New Path' in its 'Implementation Guidelines for the Rural Housing Sub Program' articulated the state's role elegantly:

> *It supports, strengthens and complements the mainstream. It facilitates and supports both individual homebuilders and communities, provides plots and loans, eases constraints, informs builders and trainers, and trains both participants and staff. It will intervene only when individual and communities cannot solve problems on their own. So while the state is the support and facilitator, the individual families will be doers and decisionmakers.*[2]

Later, we were to set out the conditions for a support and facilitating role. These conditions included: a responsibility of government to provide land, services and money for housing and in some cases, a basic provision of the house itself, for example, a shell or core; that the government accepts the principle of progressive rather than instant one-off development and is therefore tolerant of an 'unfinished' development over the longer term; that it will tolerate a wide variety of built solutions, albeit within a set of agreed guidelines – of plans, construction types, materials, finishes – whose standards are geared to individual priorities and budgets rather than determined by government; that priorities of need are to be negotiated with families and community groups, and that implementation would be locally administered, with assistance when deemed necessary; that affordability would be geared toward willingness to pay; and that the state would provide clear guidelines for this new initiative, negotiating a framework within which families and communities could act freely. That framework itself would be negotiated and developed collaboratively. It would include a housing options package with corresponding loans from government, clarifying roles and responsibilities among all stakeholders in the interest of exploring new partnership and new forms of governance; offering clear guidelines for financing programmes; establishing a continuous training or capacity building programme that would avoid providing solutions, but rather help local collectives discover the different ways in which they could meet their own needs; and provide the tools and expertise where needed to moderate these explorations.[3]

High ideals indeed, which found practical expression in both rural and urban housing programmes and in the institutional reorganization of government departments and the responsibilities of managers. Urban and rural development programmes, for example, shifted away from renewal and redevelopment and toward upgrading in both rural and urban areas. A housing options and loan package provided rural loans for a variety of construction investments – utilities, repair, extensions, and new core houses at interest rates of around 6 per cent. Substantial decentralization to local district and village councils occurred. A nationwide training programme was launched to strengthen local traditional institutions and to organize, build, manage and finance the various programmes. These included thrift societies, village organizations and community development councils (CDCs).

Various tools were developed to assist local organizations in planning, design, bookkeeping and maintenance. These included the homeowner file, which helped families control the construction and financing of improvements, as well as numerous guidebooks on how to build, organize and manage.

In 1985, housing and upgrading, until then two separate divisions in government, were integrated under the auspices of the NHDA, with some 63 staff transferred from the Urban Development

Authority (UDA) to the NHDA. Responsibilities for formulating, implementing and managing programmes were decentralized to the NHDA's district offices. In rural programmes the Gramodaya Mandala or village-level based administration became an active partner in deciding needs within community; and in urban programmes, CDCs, elected bodies of community members, were set up to promote the 'reawakening of self-confidence' among people, harnessing local resources and ensuring local needs were understood and met.

As the rural and urban programmes emerged, it became increasingly evident that housing was just one element of a broader agenda of improvements – of health, education, land tenure and social development, including issues of social and sometimes ethnic exclusion. A new breed of NHDA project officers emerged, acting as go-betweens, mediating between the needs of the NHDA, the district offices, the Gramodaya Mandala and families.

Our own task at MIT throughout this process was to introduce these new initiatives, their methods, tools and techniques, which were to become integral to participatory practice. At first, these approaches were grouped under the rubric of 'making microplans' – a series of field-based action research programmes designed to train officials and community groups in the 'new approaches' and to jump start the improvement process on site. Later these processes became known as Community Action Planning (CAP).

The scope of work and size of the settlements that piloted these programmes varied. They included sites and services projects, piloted with Navagamgoda at Baseline Road in Colombo (see Chapter 9) and upgrading. In all cases, the workshops included CDCs, NHDA representatives, including the project officers, representatives of the district's municipal councils, including health officers, engineers, land surveyors, as well as representatives of local NGOs and donors. Gothami Road in Colombo, for example, was a settlement of some 250 families living on state-owned land, bordered by a canal on one side and blocks of NHDA flats on the other. It was the first of a series of micro-planning workshops, which identified a wide range of priorities for improvement: land fill and drainage; repair of existing houses; health information; street lighting; adult education; toilets; repair of water lines; and land tenure.[4]

At Nugagahapura, there were some 64 families living in 54 units of a 30-year old informal settlement with a range of issues, only few of which fell within the conventions of physical upgrading (the need for permanent housing, land tenure, improved drainage, street lights, toilets). Of greater priority to local groups were pre-maternal health, unemployment, mosquitoes, school drop-outs, drug addiction, child nutrition, the need for savings and family health planning. The need for interagency coordination as well as the search for catalysts to get the process going without getting bogged down became key issues, the first challenge to our understanding of how to disentangle practical and 'now' interventions from longer-term strategic ones, and importantly, how the former might be a first step in achieving the latter.

The Sri Lankan programme had avoided simplistic problem-solving techniques, recognizing the complexity of shelter as a system involving people, actions, intentions and events. Sri Lankans recognized that their programme, if it was to work as a support paradigm, had to strike a careful balance (always shifting from place to place and from time to time) between community needs and governmental objectives; between adequate off-site preparation and on-site development and implementation; between the need to know, to inform action and the desire to act, to build knowledge and experience.

While these programmes ended formally in 1989 with a change in government, their legacy nevertheless is significant. Like Adelaide Road, the Sri Lankan programme was part of a movement of planning reform, a global movement demonstrating the processes of housing and urban improvement, and of exploring what these might mean, technically and organizationally, sparked by the political will to change the expectations of what planning can and should deliver and to experiment with new paradigms, not just new techniques. Importantly, it created the kind of political space that consolidated the CDCs as partners in local governance; it opened opportunities for new initiatives to develop – for example, the Women's Bank – and it provided incentives for new NGOs to emerge and grow.

NOTES

1. Most of my data are drawn from 'Housing mainstreams – A case study in learning,' an unpublished paper prepared by Susil Sirivardana for the National Housing Development Authority of Sri Lanka (n.d.). For further reading, see Disa Weerapana (1986) 'The evolution of a support policy for shelter – The experience of Sri Lanka,' *HABITAT International*, 10(3) (a clear and succinct presentation of how the Million Houses Programme policy was developed). Also see Susil Sirivardana (1986) 'Reflections on the implementation of the MHP', *HABITAT International*, 10(3) (an overview of implementation written in September 1985 that documents the pilot phase during 1983 to 1984).
2. Slettebak, A. (1986) *Learning From Sevenagama: Insights into Aspects of Support-Based Rural Housing*, A joint publication of the NHDA/MIT Research Program, Cambridge, Massachusetts.
3. Hamdi, N. and Goethert, R. in cooperation with Susil Sirivardana and Disa Weerapana (1983) *Housing Options for Sri Lanka: A Program of Opportunities for Settlement Design*, A joint publication of the NHDA/MIT Research Program, Cambridge, Massachusetts.
4. Goethert, R. and Hamdi, N. with S. Gray and A. Slettebak (1988) *Making MICROPLANS: A Community-Based Process in Programming and Development*, IT Publications (Practical Action Publishing), Rugby.

9

CASE FILES:
LEARNING FROM PRACTICE

On 8 December 2013, I met again with Jaya to get his overview of progress and to understand when and how he had set up Sevenatha, an NGO working in poor communities everywhere. Our broader interest was to review progress with projects and programmes that had been started in the 1980s and some of the post-tsunami housing, to confirm or otherwise lessons learned internationally.

I had known Jaya during the days of his tenure with the NHDA. Now in December 2012, we sat in the courtyard of the Havalock Place bungalow, in the steaming heat of the early evening. He gave me his own version of history, before we went out to look and listen and learn of his progress. Jaya's interests in housing and participatory practice were first sparked by his involvement in Soli Angel's 'building together' housing project in Bangkok in 1981. His first government posting in 1983 was with the slum and shanty division of Sri Lanka's UDA. In 1985, urban upgrading and housing were integrated into a single unit under the NHDA's Urban Housing Division. Jaya's work focused at that time in the areas known as a Wanathamulla (now called Sevilipura). Using the CAP methods he had acquired through our earlier training programmes, he applied them first to the regularization of land, working with the community through the CDCs, which he had helped build, and to sort out titles, boundaries, public access ways – to give security of tenure, provide loans and build up infrastructure. In 1989, with the change of government, there was a significant ideological shift away from participatory planning and back to direct construction. Jaya left the NHDA in 1990 and joined the University of Sri Jayawardenepur as a senior lecturer while at the same time, continuing his work in communities. His ambition was to continue the momentum of his CAP work, despite changes in governmental policy and to use his skills as a mediator and his contacts to negotiate with government on behalf of the CDCs.

In 1990 Jaya started Sevenatha in order to consolidate his action planning work and to sustain the initiative of the Million Houses Programme at the local level. His first project with Sevenatha was to put together a community contract for building individual toilets, starting small, starting with practical needs yet big ambitions. At the time, Jaya was working with a Japanese volunteer. Under the Japanese Embassy's small grants programme, they had secured a grant of $25,000, which got the project started in Gajabapura community. People built their own individual toilets and made connections to a common septic tank built by the CDC. Sevenatha provided the expertise and trained a series of community experts in sanitation. The programme was successful enough to secure a second grant from the Japanese Embassy, with which they were able to scale up their first initiatives. As the news of the success of these first projects got around, there was more demand and for Sevenatha, an enhanced reputation. Their success attracted the attention of the World Bank, UN Habitat and other donors. They practiced the ideals founded in participatory practice. Jaya's entrepreneurship enabled him to work with government authorities, the Japanese government and UN agencies, which was the foundation of Sevenatha's success. They started with a practical need for toilets, but were clear about the bigger purpose – to empower local communities to have voice in deciding their own needs and meeting their own aspirations.

Today, Sevenatha starts with big purpose and their partners are many. We visited a workshop on 9 December 2012 at Mihindi Marawata, held in an old school hall. It was entitled 'Empowering Colombo's Urban Poor to Realise their Right to Adequate Living Conditions,' conducted in a partnership between Sevenatha, the Women's Bank and Homeless International (UK). Its purpose in part was to revive the CDCs – to re-engage with communities.

The community of 32 families in some 26 houses were uncertain about the government's intention for relocation. The action planning workshop prioritized a number of key issues: land ownership; drainage; the need for individual rather than communal toilets; and the need for streetlights.

Importantly, they were able to present a collective vision for their community – adequate housing, access to education and health, a society without drugs and respect for differences in religion and culture within the community.

On reflection, Jaya was confident in his conclusion. The principles of the Million Houses Programme and the methods it pioneered – its ideals more so than its programmatic details – have been sustained in various ways: in the continuity provided by Sevenatha and others in the CAP methods and their underlying principles; the growth of CDCs, which continue to be integral to urban governance; the political space it opened – the Women's Bank, for example, grew in the very settlement where Jaya had first worked under the auspices of the Million Houses Programme – Wanathamulla – where its offices are still located today. And it made space for organizations such as Sevenatha to emerge and grow.

The following days, we went to visit and review some of the projects and programmes from those early years as well as others built more recently in response to more recent demands for relocation and in response to the tsunami. Our intent: to draw new lessons, or have old ones confirmed. For the purposes of our evaluation, we used the three recurring and cross-cutting themes that we identified in Chapter 5, themes that evidence from everywhere suggests underpin the success or failure of projects and programmes – good organization, ownership and the ability to accumulate and retain assets, individually and collectively. Together these three conditions of good practice, cultivated as they must be through participatory work, enable us to achieve the global agenda for action in relieving poverty and creating a fairer society. They are fundamental to improving governance, building resilience and reducing vulnerability. Evidence everywhere also confirms that the most sustainable programmes are those not where organization was imposed, nor where ownership or assets had been gifted, but rather, when all had emerged progressively, negotiated in participation – the result of open dialogue in which all stakeholders were continuously engaged, beyond the inception stage of the programme.

What do we mean by organization, what kind of ownership and how best to ensure that each practical intervention contributes in some way to asset building? Where and how was this achieved, and where not? We went to look, listen and learn.

NAVAGAMGODA

At Baseline Road in Colombo, our first stop, a vacant site bounded by the St Sebastian Canal on one side and the busy Baseline Road on the other, we were to pilot a sites and services approach to housing. A number of layout options were considered with plots of various sizes, arranged in clusters, housing some 20 to 30 families in each (Gamgoda). Initial services included standpipes and latrine blocks – one set per cluster. The relatively high value of land adjoining Baseline Road meant that it would be sold for private development in order to cross subsidize the project. At the centre of the site were to be built a school and community centre to serve the area, built first and which we then used for our community planning and other training workshops. Some sites were provided with core houses to be extended, others with shells to be adapted, most were vacant.

As the site began to consolidate in the mid-1980s, various issues became quickly evident. The CDC appointed by the Housing Authority, as it turned out, was not entirely representative of the community. When negotiating streetlights, for example, those clusters that were first served were those in which the CDC representatives lived, creating divisions within the community and raising early on a need to revisit the type and make up of organization best suited to the site, setting standards and managing development. Some, those who could not afford to build their dwelling all at once, built incrementally. The government, however,

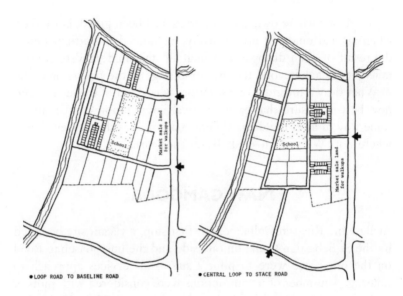

Figure 9.1 *Navagamgoda site planning options (1983)*
Source: Drawing by Brad Edgerly

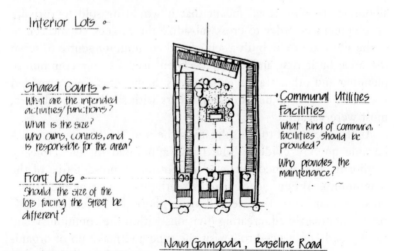

Figure 9.1a *Cluster plan (1983)*
Source: Drawing by Brad Edgerly

Figure 9.2 *Shell houses (1984)*

would only release loans after each phase of construction had been completed, which required families to upfront money, which many could not afford. Local suppliers of building materials quickly emerged who would offer materials on credit informally, sometimes at a premium.

In other cases families were able to negotiate with each other on the location and therefore the size of their plots. In one case, for example an extended family was able to negotiate three adjoining plots onto which they built a single building, housing themselves and a restaurant.

In another case, one family owning a bullock and cart that they would rent out, were initially allocated a small plot adjacent to the

Figure 9.3 *Self-build (1985)*

Figure 9.4 *Site consolidating (1986)*

Figure 9.5 *Site consolidation (1986)*

Figure 9.6 *The restaurant house (1986)*

Figure 9.7 *Navagamgoda (1986)*

more commercially viable spine road, but not large enough to house their bullock and cart. They negotiated a swap with another family for a larger plot adjoining the canal, who were happy with the smaller yet more commercial location where they would open up a shop.

It was not long before tea stalls, kitchen gardens, video parlours, in addition to all the manufacturers of building materials, would appear. It was quickly a vibrant and productive community. And yet, confirmed early on were the lessons already learnt elsewhere: that the informal market, vibrant as it was, needed regulating in order that those who were poorest should not pay a premium for materials, services and utilities; that the opportunity to negotiate priorities had also to be moderated in order to avoid minorities, those in most need, waiting longest for housing, services and utilities, or being excluded altogether from decision making; that flexibility to negotiate location and size of plot should be encouraged, first by ensuring adequate variety available on site and second facilitated by the housing authority; that the kind of community organization one works with in the initial design and planning of the site may not be effective later in managing its development, as we shall see in the example below.

We were also to have confirmed what many had already discovered: that the poor do not have enough free time to get involved according to some idealized vision of participatory planning; that their irregularity of income seriously effects the mode of construction and that few could stick to payment schedules on loans, nor afford the standards to which they were often required to build; and for the same reasons, deadlines and target dates demanded for completion of work, a requisite for releasing loan instalments, were difficult to maintain.[1]

Today, on our visit some 25 years later, Navagamgoda was dense with commercial activity, with shops, home-based enterprises, repair workshops and the rest. There were now a high proportion of renters and absentee landlords. Houses had been expanded, some with 100 per cent plot coverage, and others built up two or three stories.

Figure 9.8 *Navagamgoda (2012)*

As we walked into one cluster and talked with people more issues became evident, more lessons confirmed. What were once places of collective activity (gardens, washing, play) had become occupied, it seemed, by private enterprise, albeit informal. In one place there was a rickshaw parking lot. It had been appropriated substantially by the owner of some six rickshaw vehicles that he would lease on a daily basis to city drivers. In another corner space there was a small private dwelling on public land – an extension to an existing house opposite, constructed without agreement and now rented. While many dwellings were now connected to mainline sewers, some were not. Public latrines therefore were still in use, poorly maintained and in disrepair. The Asian Development Bank is to provide finance to build septic tanks and sewer lines for individual connections. Sevanatha will be working with local people in the design and planning of the project, which will benefit some 200 families. The lack of maintenance everywhere raised more questions about organization and about ownership.

What was lacking it seemed, were cluster-level organizations representing those that owned and those who rented to safeguard against private occupation – to safeguard the commons – and set standards and guidelines for development. Each cluster organization would elect a representative to sit on an area-wide CDC and their authority formalized by the city's municipal council. What had been provided at Navagamgoda, what it had enabled and how it had all adapted, was working well. What was now needed was the kind of organization that could respond to current circumstances, working in partnership with the local authority to sustain progress. What was also needed were alternative forms of ownership of land to be explored – land trusts, cooperatives for example, in order to sustain a sense of belonging for the longer term.

THE MISSING LIGHT BULB

Our second stop was a three-story block of flats, occupied by families of varying sizes and mixed incomes. It was the gift of the

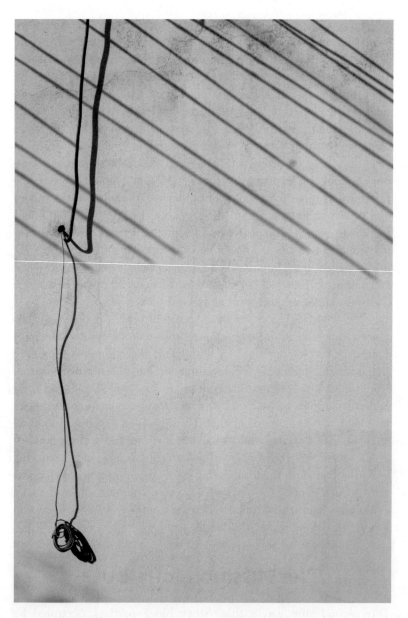

Figure 9.9 *The broken light fitting – public or private?*

Figure 9.10 *Broken railings – who maintains?*

Porsche Car Company and Eurocars Ltd to house families, some displaced after the tsunami.

Our attention was immediately drawn to the public landings and open public stair access ways, which were in general disrepair. The iron railings already rusting, some broken away and unsafe, peeling paint everywhere. Outside each of the flats on each landing there was a light bulb socket, with each light bulb missing. Other light fittings were dangling at the end of wires, pulled it seemed from their wall housings.

At night the landings were dark, and given the condition of the balustrades, sometimes dangerous, we were told. We asked one family why they had not replaced the light bulb. Their answer was simple. The light fittings on each landing were wired into each flat's private electricity meter: why should we pay for public lighting? Would it not serve both their own interests, we asked, as well as the interests of their neighbours, to replace the bulbs? Their responses were predictable. The block was still in public ownership – it was the authority's responsibility to deal with public spaces. Besides, they had been waiting for their title deeds and none had yet been decided. There was no sense of community, no sense of belonging or collective ownership, because no one could be bothered to get organized, to commit time and effort when they weren't sure if they could stay. Dependency breeds resentment because, as is typical, you cannot as an authority continue to provide what people now depend on you to provide. The result is a social and financial burden on everyone, including the local authority.

I recall the example of the street dwellers of Bombay – who some 28 years ago started Mahila Milan: these pavement dwellers pioneered savings groups, championed the cause of street dwellers against eviction and negotiated their own housing solutions. They surveyed their own street dwellings and used the information to begin a dialogue with the authorities. They were organized. Their surveys dispelled the image of beggars and thieves and instead showed the dweller's contributions to a much-needed city service. Their constant evictions solved nothing other than to move them on to other locations. In 1997, after years of activism, negotiation and organizing, their status was accepted as legitimate city dwellers. They were housed some 5000 households all together, in new building blocks. The buildings themselves, although relatively new, were beginning to deteriorate, having been trashed by squatters. Each of the 41 blocks was formed into a cooperative, which had its own community organization and community culture.[2]

What was provided at Kandaparmulawata was a building block. What was needed was more organization and clear ownership – a clear distinction in role and responsibilities between public and private – to take care of public space in partnership with the local authorities – to fix the light fittings and provide light bulbs. The developers had wrongly assumed, as they had in the old days, that building houses, if you build enough quickly enough, would be enough.

THE LIVING ROOM ON THE LANDING

In another block on the same site, another example of ambiguous ownership, another deeper example of dependency. In the absence of a collective responsibility, one family on the first-floor landing had dismantled the wall separating its private domain from the public landing. The family was relatively well off and had also extended its living room onto the frame provided for extensions at the front. As we walked up and onto the landing, it was no longer clear in whose ownership it was. It was certainly a spacious arrangement – the flat full of light and air and well furnished.

As we stood to look and listen, Sima, a mother with her two children came up onto the landing, on their way to the second floor. It seemed at first an awkward encounter – like someone walking through your living room to access his own house. I had first thought that they were part of the same extended family – an excellent arrangement of living together but separately. When we later talked to the family on the second floor, the arrangement was not as we had thought. The family on the first floor had extended their ownership onto the public landing at the expense of others. The family on the second floor was powerless to intervene. They had neither ownership

Figure 9.11 *The living room on the landing: extension of flat*

of their own apartment nor the political clout, on their own, to do anything. They had become dependent in two ways: on the local authority and on the family on the first floor, who effectively controlled their access. Despite the relative security of housing, they now felt more vulnerable than in the old days when living in their informal and illegal settlement, because in the old days before relocation, they were able to mobilize the support of neighbours and the newly formed CDC. Now they had been dispersed into what seemed to be secure surroundings, but were less secure in most ways.

The story of their displacement and arrival was familiar and shared by many we talked to. A few days earlier we had sat with three women at the headquarters of the Women's Bank in Wanathamulla and listened to their story of displacement. Shana sat at our table with two colleagues, dressed in their orange saris (the Bank's members are colour coded – orange for housing, yellow for health, etc.). They had been relocated from a place called 'Model Farm,' where they had lived for 30 years, with some 80 other families. They had no formal titles, had lived in a self-built single-story house, sometimes with two families sharing a single house. Many were members of the Women's Bank and had secured loans for improving their housing, which they had to continue to pay off, despite relocation. They had been given one week's notice before being relocated into 'transit' accommodation – a series of row houses built of timber frames, plywood walls and corrugated asbestos roof sheeting – two rooms for themselves and their five children, and a kitchen extension which they had built for themselves.

For the two years they were in transit, they were both socially and economically insecure and had no idea about tomorrow. The new location 'in transit' had disrupted the children's schooling, because you needed proof of residency to attend, which they did not at first have. The public latrines and water taps were located at the edge of the transit camp and everyone felt insecure to travel the distance at night. They had lost the social protection afforded them in a community.

Now in their new place, Sima, like Shana, was little better off, despite the better physical conditions. There were rumours that new charges would be levied in order that the local authority, who was now responsible for management and maintenance, could recover costs and provide the services needed to maintain the public areas and the fabric of the buildings – the burden of gift, it seemed, on everyone.

THE TAILOR'S WORKSHOP

In other places (post-tsunami villages) there was lots of evidence of getting it wrong with respect to design, planning and the way in which public or charitable interventions were directed. The signs everywhere give it all away, some a constant reminder of gift and securing the identity of the charitable (Figures 9.12, 9.13, 9.14).

Figure 9.12

Figure 9.13

Figure 9.14

Many people we talked to were resentful rather than grateful for what had been provided. Shoddy buildings, where contractors had saved on materials, party walls that were too thin, neighbouring toilets that were visible from adjoining bedroom windows, inappropriate kitchens, rotting window frames as no preservative had been used, blocked gutters, warped doors. And as we had seen previously, fragmented communities with no incentive to organize, given the uncertainty of tenure.

Then there were playgrounds that had become derelict for lack of care, some now used for hanging laundry; community centres only partially used or not at all; and poor settlement location – away from work and from schools and markets.

One young family told of the stress and disruption of daily life. The husband, a fisherman, had relocated to the coast for most of the week for convenience of work. She was faced with the daily school run of more than 12 kilometres each way. The family

Figure 9.15 *Playground or laundry space?*

income was partly dependent on their family shop, which she ran at the front of their house, which she could not maintain easily, given the time it took to get to school and back each day. To save on bus fares, she had taken to staying in town and waiting for the end of the school day to bring her children back home. She had managed during that time to find part-time cleaning work at nearby households, but that's not what she wanted to do.

It was Arif Hasan who, in his studies of eviction and relocation in cities everywhere, concluded that relocation undermines family assets and particularly of women, on whom many household incomes depend, because of the time and money it takes to get to work, which often is equal to – if not more than – the income that can be earned.[3] It all lacked a collective organization in land ownership and rendered one's assets vulnerable.

And then there was talk everywhere of corruption – or the perception, at least, of corruption – and of the unfair distribution of houses. Houses gifted to victims but co-opted by government to hand out to others for political or other favours, some directed to the market for profit. Some families had registered individual family members as separate households and had acquired two, sometimes three houses – one of which they occupied, the others they rented. And yet, we have learnt from the old days of social housing in countries everywhere, the more you build, the more demand you create – the more families register as separate households, the longer the waiting lists. And as standards improve, so are expectations raised, for better standards and more houses.

Others on our visits had moved back to their villages, rebuilt their houses and had rented their gifted house to tenants. In another house was a tailor and his enterprise. The house, for which they were waiting its title, was used in its entirety for shirt-making. In one room was a warehouse of pinstriped shirts, ready for delivery; in another a line of sewing machines and in yet another, rolls of material of different qualities and colours, ready for tailoring. On the ground floor was a place for relaxation and for food for him and his co-workers, and for him to spend the occasional night. The man had been a tailor for over 20 years and employed 8 people from

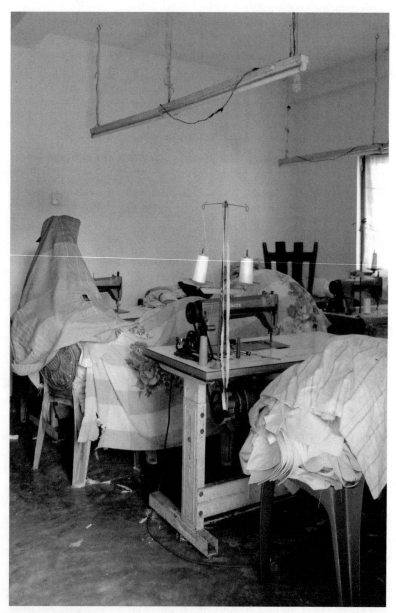

Figure 9.16 *The tailor's workshop*

outside the village. His previous factory and store had been destroyed. The house had been given to his aunt after the tsunami, who had returned to her land and rebuilt the family home for both herself and the tailor's family. They were all delighted with the gift with which they were rebuilding their livelihoods.

Were these practices corrupt or unfair? Or were they ingenious ways of using your gifted house, of turning it into an asset? I looked up the definition of 'corrupt' in my 1934 Oxford Dictionary: 'Rotten, depraved, wicked, influenced by bribery.' By this definition, the practices we had observed were not corrupt. I searched for a broader definition of corruption, one with moral value, and found it in Laurence Cockcroft's Book, *Global Corruption – Money, Power and Ethics in the Modern World*. In it he suggests that corruption 'always involves the acquisition of money, assets or power in a way which escapes the public view, is usually illegal, and is at the expense of society, as a whole, either at a "grand" or everyday level.'[4] Were the kind of practices we were observing escaping the public view? Were they at the expense of society as a whole or everyday life? Were they illegal? I could not decide!

Back in the field, in search of catalysts with which to rebuild community and livelihoods, more evidence of ways of rebuilding the commons, growing opportunities for enterprise and social development, recognizing the collective advantages in, for example – growing food. Everywhere in places we visited people were growing food, mostly at a very small scale in home gardens, in cans and buckets, even in gutters, occasionally in allotment style on public land. People everywhere proudly pointed to their successes and to the improvement each was making to the street life and to the image of the street as a desirable place to gather. What if one was to mobilize a new collective around food – well tried and successful in numerous other places – the Soil for Life organization for example, in Cape Town or Cultivate in Oxford.[5] Food sharing as a catalyst for development, in addition to its obvious practical advantages when grown locally, has a number of longer-term strategic advantages as well. It can be a catalyst socially:

> *by empowering individuals the building of a collective responsibility…Economically – by giving the opportunity to produce and participate in the informal economy and on a larger scale, giving access to formal markets; ecologically – by organizing organic waste, improving soil fertility, absorbing storm water into the biosphere and improving the microclimate; spatially – by adding long-term qualities to neighborhoods, livelihood and individual property; educationally – as a tool with which to raise awareness about how to change one's situation and by generating a sense of meaning for everyday actions; health – by activating people, giving them basic nutrition and letting the production of food have a crucial role in the attainment of a better quality of life.*[6]

In all these ways and through the participation of local people in partnership with other institutions, public and private, resilient organizations can be built, cultivating ownership socially and economically, and building all kinds of assets:

> *In the gap between public, civil and market involvement exists an unutilized potential for change. By creating and strengthening intermediate physical and social spaces where people and innovations can meet – new relations, collaborations and deals can emerge. Individual initiatives and actors could connect with each other in the local community and other parts of the city, creating a sense of reciprocity that is spread in the community. The creative outcome of these new relationships is hard to predict – something that makes the urban system dynamic, fast moving and propagating multiple perspectives, ideas and innovations.*[7]

NOTES

1 See for example: Benjamin, S. (1985) *Towards Responsive Projects & Programs: Lessons from a Site and Services Project*, A joint publication of the NHDA/MIT Research Program, Cambridge, Massachusetts.

2   See: ACHR (2013) 'Pavement dwellers in Bombay move to new homes,' Asian Coalition for Housing Rights (ACHR) e-news November 2012 to March 2013, Bangkok.
3   Hasan, A. (2006) 'The changing landscape of Asian cities: The case of Karachi,' *Journal of Research in Architecture and Planning*, 5. For a comprehensive understanding of the causes and impacts of evictions, see *Forced Evictions – Towards Solutions?*, Second Report of the Advisory Group on Forced Evictions to the Executive Director of UN-Habitat, Nairobi.
4   Cockcroft, L. (2012) *Global Corruption: Money, Power and Ethics in the Modern World*, IB Taurus, London, New York.
5   Palmer, H. *et al.* (2012) *Change Making, Dealmaking, Spacemaking: Notes on Cape Town*, Royal Institute of Art, Stockholm.
6   Palmer, H. *et al.* (2012) *Change Making, Dealmaking, Spacemaking: Notes on Cape Town*, Royal Institute of Art, Stockholm.
7   Palmer, H. *et al.* (2012) *Change Making, Dealmaking, Spacemaking: Notes on Cape Town*, Royal Institute of Art, Stockholm.

PART 3 SUMMARY: THINGS TO THINK ABOUT

For society, attacking the evils of inequality cannot alone generate mutual respect...the nub of the problem we face is how the strong can practice respect toward those destined to remain weak.

Richard Sennett

In Part 3 we looked to ways of cultivating the political and policy environment in order to create conditions for change, specifically in respect of the design, delivery and management of housing and the housing environment. We went back to evaluate a number of projects in Sri Lanka according to our three themes of organization, ownership and asset building.

Cultivating the top entailed at least the following. First, converging political ideals with practical realities, vested political interests with public interest goals and showing how these can be achieved, political expediency with innovation — a chance to lead on a global level. Second, cultivating the top entailed changing mindsets, changing habits and behaviour among authorities, modifying attitudes, engaging with power holders, seeing government in a support role providing what needs to be provided in land, services, money, training to enable human development and not just an adequate supply of housing.

Third, there was the need to reflect all this into new policy, creating the conditions for a support role; accepting progressive rather than instant development; tolerating variety and negotiating diversity as a measure of efficiency rather than standardization; recognizing the complexity of housing as one component of wider development, when it comes to upgrading, which might also include issues of health, employment, education, child nutrition; ensuring that priorities are negotiated among stakeholders in what came to be known as CAP workshops. Fourth, these policies were crafted into programmes and delivered at a variety of levels. There was, for example, the housing options and loans package, the training and capacity-building programme, the move to more upgrading and less redevelopment, less displacement. Fifth, both policies and programmes demanded a measure of institutional reorganization of those involved in housing and urban development – greater interagency coordination, the convergence of some housing responsibilities, in cities, the CDC and in rural areas, the village development councils or Gramodaya Mandale.

In case files some new lessons were learnt and mostly old lessons confirmed. With Navagamgoda and the Rickshaw Park were the obvious need for cluster-level organization to safeguard against the private occupation of public land and the need to explore new forms of land ownership. The lack of continuity in support policies coupled with a significant rise in rentals has undermined a collective commitment to wellbeing.

In the case of the missing light bulbs, lack of tenure, muddled public and private territory and responsibility, the lack of collective forms of negotiation and decision making, all undermined a sense of belonging and therefore a commitment to get organized and take ownership. The visible deterioration of place was in evidence everywhere. In the case of the living room on the landing was a similar set of circumstances and in addition, the clear need for a more hierarchical organization to moderate the more powerful in community who were appropriating public space for private gain. The story of the family on the second floor gave an example of how displacement had undermined their social and financial assets, despite their previous informality, and confirmed that legal tenure (albeit yet to be confirmed) and improved housing conditions on their own do not add up to improved wellbeing. In the example of the tailor's workshop we questioned the ethics of how housing was allocated in post-tsunami reconstruction and indeed, the ethics of turning public assets – albeit gifted to victims – into private gain.

Finally, in the case of food growing we sought out clues with which to start to build collective responsibility, a social economy, a catalyst with which to get organized, empowering individuals, encouraging participation in the local economy, collecting organic waste and improving soil fertility, adding value to underused spaces, raising awareness among all about nutrition, the environment and the opportunities both implicit and explicit in food production.

Part 4:
Enablement and the Art of Improvisation

*I don't agree with your argument,
but I accept your right to it.*

Aiden Ricketts

PART 4

ENGAGEMENT AND THE ART OF IMPROVISATION

Introduction

In my concluding chapter of *Small Change* (Playing Games – Serious Games), I offered a code of conduct for teaching and practice, given the mess and inequality we confront in development work, the speed at which we have to work, the competing vested interests we nearly always confront and the difficulties we seem to have in measuring our success. Its tenets are common sense: working backwards in process, in order to move forward more quickly and more visibly; starting where you can, which often means not necessarily where your priorities lie; never saying 'can't' – starting where you can; recognizing your ignorance, working somewhere in between not knowing and knowing enough; imagining first, reasoning later, releasing the imaginative, intuitive, insightful creative side of the brain, ensuring that aspirations as much as reason drive your search for better futures; embracing serendipity, giving chance a chance; looking for multipliers, building value chains; being reflective, celebrating the glory of wasting time – creatively ('what is this life so full of care if you had no time to stand and stare.'[1]) In the following chapter, we consider a number of additional themes with respect to the above and add three more codes: finding opportunity in ambiguity; 'yes is more,' insiders out and outsiders in; and the co-production of knowledge.

Note

1   See: Priestly, J.B. (1941) 'When work is over,' *Picture Post*, 4 January.

10

EMBRACING SERENDIPITY: FINDING OPPORTUNITY IN AMBIGUITY

The meeting with the Flatsdown community was due to start after lunch, organized by the conference conveners to coincide with the mainstream activities of the conference itself. The intent was to take advantage of all the dignitaries assembled from around the world from a variety of disciplines – architects, planners, anthropologists, artists – and brainstorm with residents and retailers ideas for regenerating Flatsdown.

Beryl, who was chairing the session on behalf of residents, started with a short background on how it all started. Hers was a working-class community, like many others, developed mostly in the later years of the 1800s – rows of semi-detached two- and three-story houses, occasionally interrupted with blocks of council housing put up in the mid-1970s. Their local high street had suffered the onslaught of chain stores, displacing the many small shops that there were. With the current economic downturn, those that had survived the chains were now displaced and lay empty. Where there was a sense of pride and community there was now dereliction. There were a number of open spaces – some used for play, most disused – and now perceived as 'unsafe' for residents. Signs of unemployment were everywhere, particularly among youth. Beryl talked of the ambitions of everyone to revive the area, attract families back in, search out enterprises that they could collectively embark upon, reopen the local primary school, the disused church hall, the library. She was clear about their needs, but was less clear about the means of satisfying these needs and where best to start.

As the discussions got underway and in response to the issues, various positions among the group became immediately clear. There were those who subscribed to the technical rational response – do your surveys, get the facts, sort out your priorities, look at the options, put a master plan together, then decide the most economic and expedient fix. They would be the conventional providers of housing, services and utilities with a strong emphasis on professional and managerial skills, and more recently a belief that the market will sort it out – albeit with a lot of volunteering. In contrast, there were the radicals, who believed that most of the professional elite in the room was engaged in a conspiracy against the public – the kind of people who believe that nothing can be solved without changing the whole system. They represent some of the more persistent troublemakers whom we will visit later. There were the populists – the enablers – who also believed in the conspiracy of professionals and government officials but who know that, if enabled, people can and should do something now, albeit in partnership with governments and experts. There were others who also shared a mistrust in the over-professionalization of solutions but saw opportunity in the arts, in community work, in small change – start where you can – find a catalyst and put it all together incrementally.[1]

As we continued our discussion, there was a general desire among the group to learn in more detail about Flatsdown – its community, its heritage, its physical resources and composition. Someone suggested that, as a first step, we needed a map of Flatsdown's urban morphology. Beryl hadn't the foggiest idea what he meant, but in any case nodded knowingly. It was her way of acknowledging her commitment and in turn being acknowledged herself.

That evening, she pondered on what he could have possibly meant. She looked up 'morphology' in her 1934 copy of the Oxford Dictionary: 'morphology – the study of the form of animals and plants,' it said. She concluded that he must have been some avid eco-warrior – a green fanatic intent on saving the world. She had met many in her days of campaigning for community voice, many of whom were their own worst enemy given their activism and tree-hugging habits, despite their good intent.

That evening after Bingo, Beryl got together with her friends and fellow campaigners and mapped in as much detail as they could all the green and wildlife characteristics of the area. It was in its own right a process of self-discovery, given that they had given little thought to 'green' in the face of all their other pressing problems.

When Beryl presented her morphological map the following day, it surprised everyone. The information on tree types, plant life, soil conditions, bird life – on where foxes had been spotted – was impressive in its mapping of natural resources but not what the assembled architects and planners had expected. There was a temptation to interrupt and acknowledge that this was not what they had meant – to start again with a plan, annotated with its streets and buildings, looking at relationships between built and unbuilt space – at lines of access and land values – at ownership patterns and vacant properties. Instead, Beryl was thanked for her presentation and in having identified an excellent starting point for regenerating Flatsdown. We would use the natural resources of the area to cultivate food, negotiating with one of the high street chain stores to use their adjacent land and with the local authority to turn derelict open spaces into productive land, albeit for the meanwhile.

It would become an enterprise – not a charity – and there are examples in cities everywhere. In Cape Town, South Africa, for example, 'Soil for Life' teaches people how to grow their own food in areas where soil fertility is poor. The objective is food production as a catalyst for social and economic development and for improvements and education in healthy eating. In Sri Lanka, Help-O's Home Garden Project, with finance from the Food and Agriculture Organization (FAO) promotes food security by encouraging families to grow food in home gardens that are then federated – small plots each contributing specific vegetables, fruits and herbs. 'Cultivate' in Oxford, England, another example, is a cooperative social enterprise in which members invest as shareholders and is registered as an industrial and provident society:

> *Being both a producer and a retailer, Cultivate acts as a bridge between growers and consumers to strengthen the local economy...*

> *Community investment provides an opportunity for local people and organisations to contribute to projects for community benefit with the expectation of a social dividend rather than just a financial return...Investors also become members of a democratically controlled organisation with an equal vote regardless of the size of the shareholding.*[2]

Cultivate's outlets include mobile vegetable vans and regular pop-up markets, as well as supplying local schools. Beryl's map had opened the door to exploring alternative forms of ownership and opportunities for new partnerships, of land and business. A misunderstanding, an ambiguity in terminology, had triggered the emergence of novelty in generating ideas, mobilizing local interests, political support and new forms of organization. Importantly, it had sparked a process, itself ambiguous, which would enable them to be a part of a global movement in reforming food production, in urban agriculture.

At first, the man from the local authority had been worried. He belonged, significantly, to those who were the technical rationalists, with a leaning to engaging the arts and community but nervous of the fuzziness of both. 'How can we start,' he had said, 'before the overall regeneration plan has been worked out, before we have done our surveys and analysed the data?' What we needed first, he argued, was a master plan to tie it all together, to give it all coherence, to get it all right. The trouble is that in the time it takes to get it all right, to develop the master plan, the chances of getting it wrong increase because circumstances change, because people lose interest and trust, because nothing tangible happens for too long. There is, in other words, a complementarity of ambiguities between meaning and process, which are both at the core of action science and action research. Both demand progressive reflection in action, which hinges on surprise and on chance, on the opportunity to stumble upon good ideas, to be flexible and entrepreneurial. What the man from the local authority was saying was you can't start before you have worked it all out; whereas our own response was, you can't work it all out until you start and then incrementally put the bigger plan together, with standards and controls as necessary to safeguard the public interest. This enables us to start more quickly and sometimes, more innovatively.

The third kind of ambiguity implied in Beryl's plan is of function – an invitation to occupy and transform spaces and places, designed or leftover, into other than what might have been intended. The occupation and transformation of open land in Flatsdown is one example. The shop under the stairs, which we visited in Chapter 3, is another of the many examples of the intelligence of informality.

All three kinds of ambiguity of meaning, of process and of function involve the need to improvise, as we have discussed in Chapter 2. The first, to make content specific terms and ideas, to make them meaningful to time and place; the second, where each action in action tells something about the next; the third, hacking into systems and places in ways that are transformative, meaningful and profitable.

Notes

1 Ward, C. (1985) *When We Build Again: Let's Have Housing that Works!*, Pluto Press, London.
2 Cultivate, 'Community Share Offer,' Cultivate, Oxford: info@cultivate oxford.org.

11

'Yes is More:' Getting Unstuck; Working with Troublemakers

Workshops, at least the kind with which I have been involved, which purposefully include all types of stakeholders, are full of troublemakers. That is, people or groups intentionally or otherwise who interrupt and sometimes disrupt proceedings. If effectively harnessed, they have much to contribute.

During the first phases of work, it is fascinating to observe the jostling for position among individuals and groups, guided often by the natural tendency in any one group or social setting to find one's place, to sort out what you stand for. Troublemakers, in particular, often struggle with the complex interplay between 'who they actually are, what they imagine themselves to be, what they attempt to appear to others and what others actually see.' While the positions are often stereotyped by virtue of one's status and work, they are constantly negotiated and modified in group work. For that reason, many group sessions are a discovery of self in relation to others – a prelude to finding out where you stand on the issues at stake – which in turn defines who you are and with whom you are likely to align.

Unlike the old days, troublemakers don't always sit at the back, easy to spot and most times, easy to ignore. On the contrary, they often cluster at the front or intermingle. They are there with purpose – to safeguard the status quo and their own status, to get what they can to promote their cause or their organization, argue a point of view to change minds, support a particular set of ideals, push for inclusion in what they might see to be an exclusive event, or simply to disrupt a process that they see as politically, economically or ideologically threatening. The trouble is that some troublemakers whom one wants to include – entrepreneurs, self-styled landlords occupying public land, self-interest minorities – don't turn up to workshops. They see these processes as cumbersome, getting in the way of the pursuit of wealth and happiness, or indeed exposing their exploitation of people and circumstances on which they depend, for money, status and political ambition. My natural tendency in the old days was to exclude these people – get them out so that we can get on with the business of planning: 'don't waste time with [troublemakers]; rather, you work with active change agents and with the vast middle ground of people who are open minded.'[1] Today we have learned that troublemakers are the very people one wants to respect and to engage in our search for appropriate responses and in repositioning questions, priorities and starting points when planning our interventions. Reaching consensus with these kinds of groups and individuals often demands, conventionally, excluding those who refuse to subscribe to the majority view, and in so doing to exclude diversity in favour of uniformity. We have learned instead that discontinuity, difference and interference are the coherence we search for in planning – to be accommodated rather than attempting to sort it all out, which can take months. And that recognizing that differences 'means respecting the views of those whose interests lead them to disagree.'[2] In any case, you don't silence dissent by exclusion; you do so by inclusion. You do it in ways that complement the consensus view. Integrating the one-off, after all, is one of the creative functions of action planning – a part of the vitality that comes with diversity. As we observed in our session with Beryl, troublemakers come in all sorts of shapes and sizes.

The most obvious and visible troublemakers are the angry – angry at the public authority for reneging on its commitment to supply affordable housing, at the new team of consultants arrived again to do more surveys with still no action, at their new neighbours and their latest venture into urban chicken farming, or at being excluded. In contrast, there are the silent ones. They cluster together in whispers and refuse to engage in debate. In this sense, they are disruptive – their silence intimidating – hiding knowledge, fearsome of commitment or exposure – protecting, often through their silence, their own self-interests, or just intimidated by the presence of others by virtue of their gender, age, class or ethnicity.

There are, of course, the talkative ones – the know-it-alls who come often with status and are polite, authoritative, sometimes patronizing. They have worked it all out and seek affirmation – shutting everyone out who interrupts, lest their own plans and opinions be interrupted. They are there to talk, not to listen. Others may neither be talkative nor angry, but cause trouble because they have already made up their minds what should be done and how. They know they will get their way in the end, because they have power and authority. They choose their moment carefully to intervene, not in group work, but in plenaries, surprising their colleagues with pre-emptive statements on what should be done and how, in order to proceed. They come with high ideals, difficult to deny – protecting society, conserving the environment, rebuilding the economy. Finally, there are those who are perceived to be troublemakers because they are seen to divert attention from the big issues decided by outsiders, but are in fact articulating a particular need that is tangible for them. The woman with the leaking roof is one example. Each of these categories of troublemakers brings to our planning information, perceptions, priorities, positions that are essential in sorting out where to start and how to proceed – sustaining development – whether in regeneration, in housing or in climate-change adaptation. How then should we unblock the path when we get stuck? How to be inclusive of those whose opinions and behaviours stand in the way or are seen to be disruptive?

One way is to neutralize dissent from the start – the pro forma way – to exclude any chance of troublemaking and therefore of discovery by ensuring clear divisions between them and us. Imagine, for example, the following 'public consultation':

At a platform an official of the housing authority explains his authority's intentions to build a large housing project. Other specialists sit with the speaker to answer specific questions if they arise. They are there because they are required by legislation. The blurb explaining the purpose of the meeting is written for the benefit of those who wrote the blurb: 'we are here to understand your needs and aspirations so that we can respond appropriately.' (We doubt we will be able to do much about either but for a short moment, we will all feel better about ourselves, and more, we will have met our legal obligations for consultation). The speaker has an electronic pointer, which he uses to pick out salient features of his new project, presented in full colour, which he flips through with the aid of his PowerPoint.

At the other end of the room sit about 40 people; some are abutters to the proposed project and others hope they will receive one of the houses being built. Also in the audience are the activists and others who are there to champion the cause of 'power to the people,' to challenge the system, and those who assume authority, however they were appointed or elected.

Few in the audience can see what the speaker is pointing at (he uses feasibility drawings done to 100th scale), and even those who can see might not understand what he is really saying because his language is obscure. 'Spatial configuration of the plan, derived on the basis of deductive reasoning,' he says. 'It is an optimally functional synthesis of user demands, based on months of surveys.' He talks of internal streets and spines instead of corridors. He knowingly hides as much as he reveals in language and in his choice of numbers and visuals.

Most of the 40 people present shuffle about impatiently; the meeting has been in session for over two hours. Some nod off to sleep, and others eye their watches nervously (it is getting late for the babysitter, the stores will close in a half hour). Finally, the speaker summarizes the salient points and turns to his experts to ask if he has missed anything. Then he asks for comments or questions from the audience. This is usually followed by a silence; no one wants to expose themselves more than they have to. Then, someone asks about safety for children, given the likely increase in traffic implied by the proposal. The speaker acknowledges the question and suggests we come back to it later (the equivalent usually of pressing the delete button on his laptop). One of the activists complains about the poor quality of sound insulation between dwellings in his own project. His comment has little or nothing to do with the purpose of the meeting, which by this time most people have in any case forgotten.

The speaker asks everyone to dream about their future by way of concluding his meeting. Another activist stands up: 'I only dream when I'm asleep,' he says. 'And it's about time we woke up.' At which point the speaker decides to wind up the session by thanking everyone for coming, by assuring them of his best services and by encouraging them to visit the town hall within the next week between the hours of 2 and 5 pm (when most will be at work) where the drawings will be pinned up in case anyone has any suggestions to modify the plans. Everyone gets up and leaves. The platform people congratulate themselves on how well it all went.

Another more reasonable way is through negotiation, facilitated in CAP workshop settings. A number of guidelines are worth noting when conducting 'principled negotiation' and that underpin the process for 'getting to yes' and the processes of action planning.

First, the importance of *separating the person from the problem*, making clear distinctions between problems as stated and the person's often emotive response to that problem. 'It's hard to negotiate effectively with a party that you have demonized.' Second, *working with other parties' interests, not their positions*. Positions are symptoms of vested interests that have to be understood, even respected. 'Conflict begins because both sides adopt opposing positions. These positions reflect a person's own limited perception of what is possible or desirable...Working with interests...allows more opportunity for mutualising or establishing common ground.'[3] Third, *inventing options for mutual gain*, brainstorming the different ways to satisfy needs, making transparent their trade-offs in time, money or political expediency, for example, which each party can assess before deciding priorities. Fourth, *using objective criteria* with which to assess the options – in particular, doing a constraints analysis when assessing each option – who or what is likely to get in the way, when and why. And then work together in dealing with constraints, looking for starters rather than 'final solutions.'[4]

A new example: the venue was an old school hall, a concrete frame building with a clay-tiled roof (some tiles missing). The building was enclosed on one side with a plastered brick wall – with two large, glassless windows covered with wire mesh to keep the birds out. On the other side, a half-wall opens to a public area with odd bits of broken play equipment – a slide, a climbing frame, a merry-go-round with washing draped over its handles. Everyone sits on those universal plastic garden chairs one can get from anywhere. Passers-by lean on the half-wall to observe proceedings. Two children run through the meeting hall in chase of a colourful butterfly. No one is disturbed. In the back of the room, two old men sit, waiting for instructions to make tea or retrieve equipment. The building was donated by some charity – built with materials and technologies difficult to maintain given the limited budget of the local education authority.

We (an expert team working with a local NGO) were charged with building an action plan to upgrade a poor settlement in the inner city and importantly, to use this as a training exercise for public officials and community leaders. There were some 30 participants whom we arranged in mixed groups of five or six around five tables. These were men and women from the community, including teachers and members of the newly established women's federation, whose task it had been to ensure the rights and wellbeing of women within their community. Public officials included representatives from the water authority, the housing department, waste management, planning and municipal works. There was a representative from the donor organization funding the project and looking to meet his own agency's agenda: maximizing participation by the community and market enablement; looking to involve as much as possible the private sector in any new initiatives, albeit in some partnership with the local authority. We divided the public officials and outsiders among the five tables, as far as possible, and got the discussion underway.

Our first intent was to get a general sense of needs and aspirations from all the stakeholders and to get organized for fieldwork – transect walks, mapping, looking, listening and prioritizing. It was also a first occasion to judge where the likely sticking points might be, whose interests dominated in the discussion, whose voice was loudest, and where some control might be needed later in deciding or modifying priorities – an initial and informal stakeholder analysis, conducted in action – good enough to get started.

After the first hour or so, the usual became quickly evident. The public officials were mostly dominating the discussions, with their monologues of what is right or wrong to do with respect to each of their specific agendas – water, sanitation, housing, waste – with occasional interventions from community members, usually male. They had done it before, they said, and there were lessons learned. The status of their experience silenced dissent and pre-empted the needs and aspirations of others. Others – women in particular – were largely silent, some chatting quietly to each other, unsure and mistrustful of where it would all lead, the women suspecting they were there to make up the 'gender balance.' We made no attempt at this stage to facilitate or to interrupt – only to observe and record, and occasionally to respond to questions with respect to clarity of purpose and process. I had learnt some time ago that using your authority as facilitator can undermine the authority of others in public or can humiliate – for example, asking someone, however politely, to 'give others a chance to speak,' – can induce resentment and sometimes anger. It singles people out and serves to reinforce the very authority that one is trying to mediate. Much better to instruct collectively, as part of training, as we would do in our next session.

The presentations by each table were predictable and sector specific. They represented the vested interests of the public officials (and sometimes the political ambitions of equally vocal community leaders at each respective table). And so, at one table, water management was prioritized as a need with aspirations to ensure both its quality and quantity – if only people followed the rules set down by the water authority (for example, no illegal tapping of mains; no selling to others for profit; no filling of tankers for door-to-door delivery). The housing official prioritized safe construction and healthy living (good foundations, permanent materials, adequate cross-ventilation, no wood fires for cooking inside the home, keeping densities within agreed limits, no encroachment on public land – none of which were affordable or doable for most who were present!). The waste official argued the need for more diligence with respect to waste management in households and neighbourhood streets, quoting the three 'Rs' of effective management – reduce, reuse, recycle. He knew that rules are there to change behaviour; power over rules is real power.[5] But he had failed to observe that most of the waste was gathered in and around public places, where the municipality was failing in its duty to collect, reuse and recycle. It had neither the capacity nor the will to collect from an area that was considered, in any case, illegitimate. The man from the education department prioritized for his group improved transportation for children to school, involving easier access for school buses into the neighbourhood – widening roads, moving some houses, and so on.

In our next session, and given what we had seen and heard, our objectives and therefore group organization shifted accordingly. In our groups, this time around, all officials were at one table, the other people at the other tables, clustering as many of the women as possible together – recognizing that the task of integration would come later, around projects and programmes in which all would have a vested interest. In this way and without intimidation, officials would have one voice at one table and the community would have five, with representatives sitting at each of the other five tables. Our objectives were threefold: first, encouraging the public officials to continue negotiating priorities among each other and coordinating their efforts unhindered by others. Indeed, some were sitting at the same table for the first time. Second, giving the silent majority not just voice, but voice with volume and in so doing, tipping the balance of need and numbers (and therefore power) in their favour. Third, ensuring that non-sector specific needs and priorities could emerge and usually from the community and subsequently, to converge the demands imposed from the top with needs and aspirations expressed from the bottom. In all three respects, we were negotiating the middle ground in between top and bottom, insiders and outsiders, one set of rationales with another.

During the presentations, the needs and aspirations of community were typically non-sector specific: improved markets for home-based industries; security of tenure; training in construction and other fields to improve employment opportunities; getting the children to school safely and more easily; managing and securing public standpipes from those who had taken informal ownership of them and were charging unaffordable fees for water; getting the elderly to clinics and hospitals more easily. Then there was the woman with the leaky roof, a troublemaker in her own right, diverting attention, an interruption for everyone – her concerns too detailed and personal at first.

During our third session, we would consider ways of integrating the sector-specific needs of each of the municipal departments represented with the needs and aspirations of community. It would entail a convergence of interests – not in the more typical and confrontational 'either or' scenario, but rather by asking, for example, how could the recycling aspiration of our waste management official integrate with the training, employment generating and market aspirations of our community? What options could we explore for mutual gain?

We then again regrouped into mixed project or programme teams – each team brainstorming ways of meeting their respective needs. How do we converge our interests without the more typical and confrontational 'either or' scenario? One basic role of brainstorming is, of course, that no one need defend their ideas and, depending on the techniques used, no one need be identified directly with any one idea – all of which encourages collective ownership of ideas brainstormed. It is the first step to exploring partnerships – to mutually reinforce each other's capabilities in the interests of a common goal. What typically emerges is innovative, sometimes ingenious: constituting tap attendants into social enterprises; building a community fund from water fees to pay the local authority and subsidize those who cannot afford to pay. The fund can also be used for other public needs, for example, investing in buckets to pick up waste. Then federating these enterprises into a neighbourhood or even city-wide organization, which through its elected members would become a partner organization to the local authority, who would offer basic training in plumbing and accounting, for maintenance and bookkeeping – all more efficient and more equitable ways of improving the management of the supply of water – everyone wins, except existing water cartels. These cartels are peacefully disbanded, security guaranteed at the top by the local authority.

Getting the kids to school safely (and the elderly to hospitals and clinics) is another typical need. This demands accessibility through the many narrow paths and roads that restrict conventional motor access for school buses, looking for alternative forms of transportation – bicycle rickshaws for school buses, for example, with locally made cabins, each able to carry six or so children; another enterprise of rickshaw drivers, a private enterprise contracted by the department of education, facilitated by our NGO partner or the Piedabus – individuals hired by the local authority to walk groups of children to school safely and informatively, relieving the burden on mothers. More employment, easier access, more efficient, more equitable, less displacement, which would otherwise result from road widening and getting the buses in.

At the local and largely disused community centre, another enterprise in waste recycling, composting and product development; training for unemployed youth in recycling waste products into household goods and even furniture, recycling paper into school exercise books and various metals into musical instruments – providing space in local downtown stores for marketing under the social corporate responsibility label – all self-organized and facilitated by the department of waste management, in partnership with the local NGO.

In all these and other examples[6] are converging interests, opening opportunities for innovations with process, techniques and partnership – processes that wind up being more efficient and more equitable because they are transparent, where partners are accountable to each other and to their respective constituents. Importantly, they are more resilient because 'the ability to self-organize is the strongest form of system resilience, the ability to survive change by changing.'[7]

Then, one guy, the planner from the municipality, champions the cause of zoning, a way in his view of tidying it all up or simplifying and making urban regeneration easier to manage and making places safer for everyone. He also knows that 'encouraging diversity means losing control,'[8] which is not his idea of efficient management. He becomes increasingly excitable and argues the need to separate into zones – residential, recreational and importantly, commercial land. His concern is, rightly, not just the settlement, but with its place in the larger conurbation of the city – attracting investment while safeguarding the wellbeing of people. The discussions become progressively more heated and antagonistic as positions (more so than interests) become retrenched, particularly among those representing all the informal enterprises so vital to the local economy. The more we argue our case for diversity, for incrementalism, for improvisation, the angrier the planner becomes. We were getting stuck.

Getting stuck means going the wrong way. Some might agree that it is the right way, but our path to achieving our goals is blocked. If your path is blocked, it is the wrong way, at least to start with. And so, one is typically faced with three options: find a different way, more messy perhaps, much longer, less rigorous but still no-less ambitious. Or you can try to unblock the blockage, because you believe the blockage to be discriminatory, a violation of rights or just inadvertently blocked by old rules and regulations, old habits, by people and bureaucracies with old ways of thinking, doing, organizing. Alternatively, you change your goals, 'attend to problems that you can attend to,' in which case one often has to compromise or worse, ignore what you believe to be right. You wind up doing the wrong thing, just because you can succeed. You wind up being a 'part of the disease and not a part of the cure.'[9] The way you decide is based as much on convictions as on ideals. The first searches out lines of least resistance – a commitment to ends because you believe them to be right, without too much concern for means, in recognition that there are lots of ways of achieving the same ends. It is more flexible and more inclusive, less confrontational. The second is a commitment to changing the means by which we achieve our ends, not because the means justify the ends, but because the way one achieves one's ends is transformative of the very systems that block progress. And in any case, because ends will always be compromised by systems that you consider to be morally corrupt, environmentally destructive or self-serving. In this case, changing the system takes precedence over achieving ends, however worthy the ends.

The question, as always, is how best to do this. Fritz Schumacher, in his efforts to promote intermediate technologies put it this way:

> *People say to me: before you can make headway with your intermediate technology, you must first change the system, do away with capitalism and the profit motive, dissolve the multinationals, abolish all bureaucracies and reform education. All I can reply is: I know of no better way of changing the 'system' than by putting into the world a new type of technology – technologies by which small people can make themselves productive and relatively independent.*[10]

In the case of our planner, we opt for searching out lines of least resistance, transforming his demand for zoning into plans that generate diversity, 'catalyzing the plans of many people besides planners' in meeting needs.[11] I have learnt from business colleagues the art of negotiating with people who block the way forward. There is the confrontational 'no' to an idea or process, which they may suggest. Then there is a more modified response of 'yes, but' – accepting an idea, but dismissing it in view of all the things that would prevent it from happening. Then there is the conditional 'yes, if' or 'yes, when' – saying yes without making promises, pointing out all that needs to happen before an idea can be progressed and implemented and often disqualified as taking too much time, requiring too much money or too much change in policy. Then there are the transformational powers of 'yes, and' and, of course, a more straightforward 'yes.' 'It's one of the ideas of "yes is more." You can be critical through affirmation rather than negation. You can be critical by putting forward alternatives rather than spending all your energy whining about the alternatives you don't like.'[12]

We diffuse the situation in our workshop with 'yes and.' We accept for the time being his demand for zoning and get him to articulate in more detail why he thinks zoning is key. In his explanation, two things become evident. First, and more difficult to dislodge, is his own entrenched position in principles of urban planning, borrowed from the pioneers of new towns and satellite towns in Britain and elsewhere and the ideals of modernists and utopian reformers everywhere (Howard, Unwin, Abercrombie, Corbusier). That is, to make places safer, cleaner, tidier and more easily manageable by local authorities and private development corporations. To do this, he was taught to segregate functions into more easily manageable bits – residential, recreational, commercial and industrial, with easy access between all. His explanation was a lesson in the tradition of modernism and a reminder of its oppressive characteristics – the city operating as a machine, with a limited number of standard building parts and a maximum of repetition to ensure efficiency – all decided by authorities and corporates at the very top. Many of these projects have been dismantled, even today; one example is La Courneuve in the West of Paris: 'What was built as a utopia has turned into a nightmare for the French, with high crime rates, rampant drug dealing, poor schools and high unemployment. Now the 200-meter long 16-story high buildings are being replaced with smaller clusters of housing.'[13] The one-size-fits-all model mostly failed to recognize that 'healthy cities are organic, spontaneous, messy, complex systems.'[14] Unlike the new urbanists who abandoned the machine analogy in favour of diversity, street life, mixed uses and with their 'small is beautiful' ethos, our planner continued to promote unknowingly the 'continuous disorder and chaos-by-design,' which he was introducing in carefully planned projects. There was no chance for surprise except for chance itself. It was Jacobs who said 'to see complex systems of functional order [in cities] as order not chaos, takes understanding' – a new way of seeing, a new paradigm:[15]

> *One of the difficulties involved in getting people, above all, planners to accept this organic complexity has been purely conventional. They*

have been taught to believe that complexity is synonymous with chaos and indecision. Thus, they assume that the contrary idea too – a simple order, the clear repetition of suburbia or new towns – is an answer to urban organization.[16]

Our planner went on to suggest that if you want to change people's habits for the better, given the density and complexities of city life today, then you adapt your behaviour and modify your expectations to fit the new and mostly unfamiliar environments of housing blocks, housing estates and shopping malls, rather than adapt your environment to your needs.

The second issue that became evident was his concern for the city as a whole – that his need was to think and plan at the city scale, with infrastructure, housing and transportation citywide. His need was to direct urban development economically and specifically in carefully controlled zones, to give it all a visual order and coherence that would attract investment, unconvinced that the best cities were never planned but were instead 'a manifestation of the freedom of countless numbers of people to make and carry out countless plans,' which Jacobs argued was 'a greater wonder' than the order of duplication typically advocated.[17]

Our planner was convinced that his master plan could be 'abstracted out of the ordinary city'[18] to attract investment, while safeguarding the wellbeing of people – but was yet unsure how to do it. His point about scale – a critique for many years of ad hoc community-driven action plans for settlement upgrading – triggered our thinking differently. What if, we thought, we stuck to his zoning ideas for now and included a new category of zone – a social enterprise zone incorporating the ideals of Howard's social city (small scale, a cooperative economy, control by community of design and land values) with Jane Jacobs' call for diversity. It would be a model of urban sustainability, a pilot that would integrate the social economy of the local with the market economy of the urban and regional. It would all be 'conceptualized' in terms of a social policy that seeks to create competitive places and new forms of citizenship, thereby allowing individual and community to 'act as both subjects and objects of policy.'[19] Sustainability in this interpretation 'becomes defined in terms of competitiveness and democracy.' New ownership patterns might be explored within these zones – perhaps an urban land trust, a form of urban commons, land not in public ownership, but with 'legal status based on rights of use, administered by an elected community development council, and incorporated into the city's governance.'[20]

Our narrative was less based on facts and surveys and the conventions of planning on which they are often derived, but more on aspiring to new futures. 'That's what story is good for. The production and scrutiny of counterfactuals (colloquially known as "what ifs") is an optimal way to test and refine one's behavior – amongst all participants.'[21]

We had already crafted the beginning of how this could work in our previous sessions. We had started with sector-specific issues, the concerns of managers and experts in each of housing, water, sanitation, education, health. In our second session we had derived from community concerns cutting across sectors, reflecting the conditions of their poverty and exclusion, for employment, markets for household-based enterprises and skills training to enhance employability. In session three, we had demonstrated how both sets of concerns could be integrated, exploring alternative forms of enterprise and partnership for managing water, recycling waste, getting the kids to school – all generating income and building ownership. We have seen how the concerns of the woman with the leaking roof, at first considered an interruption to proceedings, became a source of inspiration, generating more employment around housing and building, improving health and the life chances of children.

With the intervention of the planner, we were bound to consider a fourth and more strategic level of intervention of policy that would enable the new social enterprise zone to be integrated into the overall urban plan, giving legitimacy to an otherwise illegitimate settlement, and with it, access to resources, improving rights and entitlements, removing discrimination and encouraging power sharing through new forms of partnership for delivering housing, utilities and services. It would entail a relaxation of standards for housing that would enable incremental building and the use of alternative technologies that would be explored in what would become an urban resource centre at the once disused community centre. Other standards would be derived with community, as had been done in Thailand, for setbacks, for example, building lights, land uses, protecting the commons, thus ensuring greater compliance – standards for us, by us.[22]

As we searched for ways of getting it all started, our answer came from yet another group of troublemakers, not so far present at our workshops. They were angry because they had been excluded, a minority group known for their political activism and disruptive tendencies.

I recalled a similar event in a township in South Africa (see *The Placemaker's Guide*), where we improvised a technique borrowed from the toolkits of planning for real – the 'agree/disagree' routine. We utilized a similar technique this time around.

Everyone anonymously writes their priority on a piece of paper and places it on the table for everyone to review. If it is not your priority, you turn the paper over. Once turned, you can turn it back to look at, but then must return it face down. Of all the pieces, only one remained unturned – getting the kids to school. At first, there was dismay about how much disagreement there was and how difficult it would be to get anything done. But we had found a start – a basis for building cooperation, as we had done in South Africa.

Getting unstuck, managing constraints, accommodating the concerns of troublemakers (troublemakers often only in respect of getting in the way of what one already had decided to do, set out in our log frame, with timetables and predetermined outputs, which people were rightly challenging) had opened new opportunities not otherwise considered, because they had inadvertently demanded of everyone new paradigms – new ways of seeing, thinking, doing, organizing – which are, after all, the most profound forms of intervention, because they transform systems incrementally. We had, in other words, sought out alternative means to achieve commonly agreed ends, which themselves were derived in action. In so doing, we had begun the processes of transformation – of doing practical work, with longer-term strategic value. We had also, by means of instituting the social enterprise zone, provided a feedback loop in urban development, which would be a corrective to the self-reinforcing loop of conventional planning. It was an intervention that would modify the power of the market to self-generate instructively, which was more efficient in managing development and more equitable.

Notes

1 Meadows, D. (1999) *Leverage Points: Places to Intervene in a System*, The Donella Meadows Institute, Vermont, USA.
2 Sennett, R. (2003) *Respect: The Formation of Character in an Age of Inequality*, Allen Lane, London.
3 Ricketts, A. (2012) *The Activists Handbook*, Zed books, London.
4 Fisher, R., Ury B. and Patton, B. (1991) *Getting to Yes: Negotiating an Agreement Without Giving In*, Random House, London; Ricketts, A. (2012) *The Activists's Handbook: A Step-by-Step Guide to Participatory Democracy*, Zed Books, London.
5 See: Meadows, D. (1999) *Leverage Points: Places to Intervene in a System*, The Donella Meadows Institute, Vermont, USA.
6 See my two books: *Small Change* and *The Placemaker's Guide to Building Community*.
7 See my two books: *Small Change* and *The Placemaker's Guide to Building Community*.
8 See my two books: *Small Change* and *The Placemaker's Guide to Building Community*.
9 Schumacher, E.F. (1980) *Good Work*, Abacus, London.
10 Schumacher, E.F. (1980) *Good Work*, Abacus, London.
11 Jacobs, J. (1994) *The Death and Life of Great American Cities*, Penguin Books, Harmondsworth.
12 Parker, I. (2012) 'High rise,' *The New Yorker*, 10 September.
13 Brady, T. (2012) 'Little towns, big dreams,' *New York Times Weekly*, The *Observer*, 12 November.
14 See commentary by Eric Jaffe (2013) 'Jane Jacobs was right: gradual redevelopment does promote community,' *The Atlantic Cities*, 8 March.

15 Jacobs, J. (1994) *The Death and Life of Great American Cities*, Penguin Books, Harmondsworth.
16 Jencks, C. and Silver, N. (2013) *Adhocism: The Case for Improvisation*, MIT Press, Cambridge, Massachusetts.
17 Jacobs, J. (1994) *The Death and Life of Great American Cities*, Penguin Books, Harmondsworth.
18 Jacobs, J. (1994) *The Death and Life of Great American Cities*, Penguin Books, Harmondsworth.
19 Feinstein, S. (2012) 'Globalisation, local politics and planning for sustainability,' in Hass, T. (ed.) *Sustainable Urbanism and Beyond*, Rizzoli, New York.
20 Condorelli, C. *et al.* (2010) 'Common talking,' in Petrescu, D. *et al.* (eds) *Translocal Act: Cultural Practices Within and Across*, AAA/PEPRAV, Paris.
21 See: Eaglemen, D. (2012) 'The moral of the story,' *The New York Times Book Review*, 5 August.
22 For a full description of the process, lead by Patama Roonrakwit for the Asian Coalition for Housing Rights (ACHR), see Hamdi, N. (2004) *Small Change*, Earthscan, London, Chapter 2.

12

INSIDERS OUT AND OUTSIDERS IN: PRACTICAL WISDOM AND THE CO-PRODUCTION OF KNOWLEDGE

In Chapter 7, in our discussion on the roles and responsibilities of practitioners and institutions, I wrote that in order to become a good enabler, which I assumed to be our ambition in development work, you have to become a prudent provider. Therein lies a set of key attributes not easily acquired because they cannot be easily taught.

Hugo Slim, in his paper on practical wisdom, explores the virtues and the origins of prudence and offers a definition derived from Aristotle in his book *Nicomachean Ethics*:

> *Aristotle understood there to be two intellectual virtues – wisdom and prudence, and that 'each is the virtue of a different part of the soul.' He recognized both as distinct from each other and he also believed that they were attained in different ways. He defined wisdom as 'both scientific knowledge and intuitive intelligence as regards the things of the most exalted nature.' The wise person, therefore has great understanding and great knowledge, but it is of a high order which does not always lend itself to action, let alone right action. Of more use, perhaps, and certainly of more impact on the affairs of the world, therefore, is the virtue of prudence which Aristotle recognized is a 'practical wisdom.'*[1]

Aristotle identifies three varieties of prudence. The first he describes as 'deliberative excellence' – the ability to weigh up, analyse and so deliberate towards a right decision or choice. The second he describes as 'understanding' but an understanding that is more akin to empathy than to scientific knowledge. This perhaps is the ability to relate immediately and intimately with a situation. And third, he talks of 'consideration' or 'judgement' – the faculty of judging correctly what is just or equitable in any given situation, all of which is central to participatory practices.

Deliberative excellence, understanding and judgement are all essential in the practice of development. Deliberative excellence, because excellence can only be deliberated according to the context of issues, locally and globally; understanding based on knowledge shared between disciplines (the peer-group production of knowledge) and between different cultural norms and levels of organization; judgement, which is based on ethical considerations, on disciplinary criteria of judging quality, on interdisciplinary understanding of the interrelationships between issues and on quality of life considerations.

Deliberative excellence, understanding and judgement are also fundamental to the resilience of development practitioners, individually and collectively. That is, the ability to accommodate, adapt and transform the inner world of being cognizant into the outer worlds of becoming more relevant and more flexible, robust and skilled, all of which is essential in building the capacity to aspire and act.

Acquiring practical wisdom and becoming resilient requires that we cross boundaries and engage our own domains of thought, rationality and action as outsiders with those of others inside. I take outsiders to mean those who step outside of their own *intellectual or disciplinary* domains, outside their own *cultural or social* norms or settings, or indeed, outside of their own *levels of organization* in the hierarchy of power and decision making. Often, the challenge is to negotiate settings in which we find ourselves as outsiders in all three respects in any one setting, and doing so without becoming defensive.

Outsiders who step inside, defensive of their outside domains or big purpose, deny the opportunity for change and discovery. They will attempt to transform the inside world into which they have intervened to fit their own outside beliefs and values. In so doing, they alienate themselves from the world they are attempting to engage and revert to convention. They become manipulative, deductive and assume authority over knowledge and know-how. They deny the opportunity to acquire prudence because their excellence, understanding and judgement will have been decided normatively. 'Good decisions for them are made through explicit (and conclusive) statements of objectives and a clear view of the world…as they think it should be – which they will then impose on others.'[2]

In the classroom debate and discussion in our first chapters, we began to explore crossing boundaries by exploring the space in between learning and practice, understanding and action. We looked to ways of converging these sometimes disparate routines in our quest for cultivating practical wisdoms. Using picture analysis, we stared into the place where the woman with the leaking roof lived, seeing what we saw, then critiquing our own understanding of the value of what we were looking at – what was public, what private, where was the order and where the disorder, was it productive or counterproductive, was it deteriorating or consolidating?

In our quest for judging correctly what might be just and equitable when deciding our interventions, we began to articulate what might be ethical and what not, with all the ambiguities in between: the objective view, the moral realists, and those on the side of appropriateness and acceptability to cultural and social norms. We considered our interventions on the basis of our own disciplinary and typically sector-specific strengths, and then concluded how they might be converged in our 'discussions' of what it would take to make the place in the picture 'a wonderful place to grow up in.' We discussed the value of interdisciplinary work – doing what you do best but doing it more effectively; and taking advantage of what you do and doing more with it.

In Part 2, we explored the value of participatory work in negotiating the spaces in between typical polarities – between the freedom and flexibility of emergent structures in community whose value we enabled to trickle up and across, and the order of designed structures, which trickle down. Importantly, we argued the value of participation in converging worlds by negotiating the spaces in between differences in values, in purpose, needs and ambitions of stakeholders.

In all of the above respects, we gave consideration to the importance of crossing boundaries in order to build our practical wisdom as development practitioners. Two further considerations in the relationship between outsiders and insiders in respect to cultivating the 'knowledge commons' are worth thinking about.

First, cultivating 'peer group production of knowledge and know-how' and in so doing, facilitating processes of 'reskilling, skills sharing, building social (and other) networks, learning from others, learning from others' experiences,'[3] and learning with others. Crossing boundaries between organisations horizontally, among expert groups in interdisciplinary work, or between communities, civil society groups and local NGOs, is vital to acquiring practical wisdom at all levels, including local ones. 'Peer networks are great innovators, not because they're driven by the promise of commercial reward, but rather because their open architecture allows others to build more easily on top of existing ideas.'[4]

> *Unequal access, use and management of knowledge pose substantial threats to the common flow of knowledge and seem to undermine the capacity of weaker individuals (or groups) to innovate solutions to their own context-specific problem. Such inequality ranges from the regional dynamics between the global north and the south, to the local dynamics of class, race and gender.*[5]
>
> *Peer networks laid the foundation for the scientific revolution during the Enlightenment, via the formal and informal societies of coffeehouse gatherings where new research were shared. The digital revolution has made it clear that peer networks can work wonders in the modern age of change being driven by mass collaboration. The point is, is that when we succeed, we succeed because of our individual initiatives, but also because we do things together.*[6]

One final consideration when thinking about outsiders and insiders and our prudence in deciding interventions: as outsiders we have a double commitment – to the global agenda of issues, however we decide these, and to local ones. We recognize that in some respects, in a globalized world, issues experienced in one place are often induced in another. No better example than with vulnerability, the boundaries of which are difficult to define, whether for climate change, the violation of rights or the inequalities of discrimination. We have a responsibility, in other words, to adapt our global agendas and make them specific and meaningful locally – which is after all what deliberative excellence is about. In negotiating this space in between the local and the global, as outsiders, we have the privilege of mobility between worlds and between levels of organization. How we use that privilege will be based on our understanding of circumstances, and the courage to use our understanding in making judgements about where and how best, and with whom, to intervene, recognizing that our understanding of the complexities of place will be limited, however well we have done our homework.

One way or another, most of us will be a part of the aid industry. Our presence will likely be tainted with the agendas we bring and the status we assume, albeit often by association with one or other charity, NGO, government or international development agency. My own contention is that, with prudence, we bring at least as much as we might take. And, in participatory work, however we may bias this, our ignorance is made transparent and our intentions are negotiable.

And yet there will always be, we know, the unintended consequences of our interventions, difficult to predict, because sometimes – many times – things happen by chance, some good, some less good. Often times we take advantage of crisis, not just to build back, but to build back better. Sometimes we find ourselves, or the aid we bring, manipulated and then co-opted by people, organizations and circumstances outside of our control. Other times, we just get it wrong.

Examples are plenty. In their recent documentary 'Does Aid Work?' the BBC raised questions about the expediency of aid, for example, with reference to the famines in Cambodia. Oxfam had apparently got it wrong, it was later revealed. Four million people were not starving. Then there is food aid, often diverted in crisis, to feed the military – in Biafra, for example, or Somalia. There was the famine in Ethiopia, which as it turned out, was not the result of climate change but rather, the policy of the government to deliberately starve sectors of the populations in order to encourage their displacements, to encourage people south – a political tool, a vehicle for forced relocation. The aid agencies in this respect found themselves co-opted by political interests, despite good intentions.

Sometimes, we fuel the very crisis, the very conditions we were trying to solve. No better example than the pursuit of growth. On a global scale, a significant amount of aid goes into economic development, with a cadre of development practitioners supporting the views that 'growth, both population and economic, is the answer to everything (resource depletion, unemployment, poverty, hunger)…[But], growth has costs, among which are poverty, hunger, environmental destruction, the whole list of problems we are trying to solve with growth.'[7]

Back at the local level, in Caquete in Lima, Peru, we were working to understand the needs of street traders in a part of the city where they occupied some of the major roads leading into the city. The resultant disruption to traffic and formal commerce was significant. Occasionally, the *ambulantes* would be evicted and the streets cleared, usually by the police and the military. There was, needles to say, significant antagonism. We were there educationally as students from Oxford Brookes University working with the our counterparts at the University of Engineering in Lima to look, listen and learn – one of our annual field-based workshops for learning-in-action.

Not long after our arrival, articles began to appear in the local newspapers, championing the rights of the street traders and suggesting these rights to be also championed by the 'outsiders.' We had been unintentionally co-opted as advocates by the local and well-organized community groups and together, we opened doors for renegotiation rather than the confrontations so far evident. Over the years and on my return to Lima some years later, it was encouraging to see how land had been allocated around the city to groups of traders who had formed the equivalent of cooperatives and were trading legally and without disruption. Relocation had been negotiated.

In all these examples, good and bad, one has to decide in the end if the benefits you bring outweigh the harms you may do with your intervention. It takes prudence to decide where best and how best to intervene. It is always about trade-offs. The question is, with whom are these trade-offs negotiated and whose interests are most served? In the end, we should remind ourselves that development practitioners, 'make their own circumstances, but [often] not under circumstances of their own making.'[8]

NOTES

1 See: Slim, H. 'Practical wisdom and the education of today's relief worker,' in Hamdi, N. (ed.) (1996) *Educating for Real: The Training of Professionals for Development Practice*, Intermediate Technology Publications (Practical Action Publishing), Rugby, Chapter 16.
2 Kay, J. (2011) *Obliquity*, Profile Books, London.
3 Petrescu, D. *et al.* (eds) (2010) *Translocal Act: Cultural Practices Within and Across*, AAA/PEPRAV, Paris.
4 Johnson, S. (2012) 'The more we get together,' *The New York Times Magazine*, 23 September.
5 See: Hall, N., Hoffman, N. and Ostrowski, M. (2012) 'The knowledge commons: Research and innovation in an unequal world,' *St. Anthony's International Review*, 8(1).
6 Johnson, S. (2012) 'The more we get together,' *The New York Times Magazine*, 23 September.
7 Meadows, D. (1999) *Leverage Points: Places to Intervene in a System*, The Donella Meadows Institute, Vermont.
8 Talbot, M. (2012) 'Talk of the town,' *The New Yorker*, 16 April.

PART 4 SUMMARY: THINGS TO THINK ABOUT

> *What many visionaries have in common is their focus on the world they want to create, not on what they want to eliminate.*
>
> Boice (1992)[1]

So far, and central to the ideals argued in this book, is our search for beginnings – getting started and in process with those who know, learning more about problems and discovering sometimes unlikely opportunities. We accepted ambiguity as a condition of practice and improvised the way forward. Design and improvisation, we have argued throughout, are complementary processes, crafting synergy through participation between freedom and order, emergent structures and designed ones, unblocking the filter of knowledge and information to trickle up and trickle down. In this final part we explored further the value of ambiguity, the practice of enablement and the art of improvisation in programme development. We explored what it takes to acquire the practical wisdom necessary for enablement planning.

In Chapter 10, Beryl had embarked on a process of discovery unintended but insightful. We had stumbled on a good place to start working with community to improve the life of place and the livelihoods of its people – getting organized, exploring alternative forms of ownership, building enterprise and accumulating assets. A misunderstanding had enhanced our understanding of place. An ambiguity of meaning had triggered novelty and got things going.

In Chapter 11 our programme of work was incrementally negotiated through a series of improvised workshops inclusive of the usual mix of troublemakers. We were to discover the value of discontinuity in our search for coherence rather than consensus – the kind that is inclusive rather than exclusive, based on difference rather than sameness. In mixed groups and predictably, we gave voice and status to the talkative and self-assured, the public officials and experts – the kind who had got it all sorted, who knew where to start and how to proceed. Their vested interests, we saw, were typically sector specific, seeking after all to pursue programmes for which they were appointed to implement and manage.

In our second session, we organized into separate groups – officials, women, shopkeepers and community leaders. Our intent was threefold: to give the typically silent majority voice with volume; to enable each group to negotiate priorities among itself, with its own level of organization; to encourage non-sector specific issues to emerge, typically from community (improve markets, security of tenure, more employment, better access to healthcare and education etc.).

Our third session entailed grouping into project teams, mixed groups whose charge was to brainstorm how vested interests can be mutually served through cooperation – a 'yes is more' approach – the essence of enablement. It was a first step to innovating partnerships, making everyone accountable to everyone else.

Then and typically unpredictably, there was the zoner, fearing his loss of control over planning, arguing for more regulation, knowing that zoning is a good way of attracting investment, which was his mandate, as it turned out. His scale of thinking, his concern for the city as a whole was a corrective to our more local concerns. It triggered our thinking differently – yes to zoning, a social enterprise zone, a model of sustainability, of competitiveness and democracy. Finally the spontaneity of the angry, who gave us our starting point.

In our final chapter we considered what it took to become a good enabler, what skills and competencies might be needed to acquire prudence or practical wisdom. We gave definition to practical wisdom – deliberative excellence, understanding and good judgement. Cultivating the knowledge commons, we suggested, was key to the getting of wisdom, getting insiders out and outsiders in. We concluded by suggesting two further considerations in pursuit of practical wisdom: encouraging the peer-group production of knowledge – reskilling, skills sharing, learning from others, learning with others; and the creation of peer group networks – an open architecture of knowledge information and understanding allowing people and organizations across levels to contribute and build on what they had, and so reduce inequity, locally, regionally and globally.

Note

1   Boice, J. (1992) *The Art of Daily Activism*, Wingbrow Press, Oakland, CA, cited in Ricketts, A. (2012) *The Activists Handbook*, Zed Books, London.

INDEX

action planning: prioritizing issues 109–10; processes of 80–2; troublemakers, working with 145–9
action planning, case study: integration for mutual gain 153–4; negotiating principles 149; stakeholder interests 150–2; stalemate, alternative options 155–8; sustainability, policy options 158–61
adhocism 32
architecture: improvisation, value of 31–2; prefab housing debate 28–31
Aristotle 163–4
asset building 47–8

Bishop, Claire 58–9
Boorstein, David 67–8
Burnham, Scott 32

city organization: controlled standards 67–9, 71–2; formal and informal practices 21; inequality, effects of 22–3; inequality, planned reforms 69–72; modernist principles 157; privatized public space 65–7; visual analysis *18*, 18–20, *20*
community action planning (CAP) 105; *see also* action planning

community development councils (CDC) 104, 105, 106–7, 109–10
community enterprise: bus stop placement 77–8, 85–6; food production 78, 131–2, 142–3; public space renewal 79–80; street dwellers rehoused 122–3; street theatre (education) 80, 85; tap attendants (piped water) 78–9, 85
cross-cutting themes: asset building 47–8; buzzwords deconstructed 44–5, *45*; connected principles 45–6, *46*, 110–11; ownership 46–7
Cultivate (UK) 142–3

decisions, approaches to: action planning 80–2; disciplinary stereotypes 28; ethical considerations 25–7; expertise led 28–31, 84–5; improvisation 31–3; interdisciplinary work 33–6, *34*, 140–2
development: dealing with poverty 7; status driven 22–3, 65–6
development practitioner: codes of conduct 139; practical intervention, first step 9–12; practical wisdom 163–7;

presenting the issues 8–9; qualities of 7–8; skills needed 98–9
displacement 125–6, 135

enablement, forms of 89
environment-related disease 25, *26*
eviction, state-sanctioned 22–3, 65–6

Ferguson, Angus 35
Flatsdown regeneration 140–4
Fry, Maxwell 70

Glass House project 58
governance 59, 62–3
Greater London Council (GLC) 71, 99

Harvey, David 65
Hassan, Arif 65–6
Help-O's Home Garden Project 142
Homeless International (UK) 109
housing programmes: Greater London Council (GLC) 99; levels of assistance 111, *112–16*, 113, 117, 134–5; modernist projects 157; prefab housing proposal 28–31; Sri Lankan redevelopment 102–7

improvisation, value of 31–3
India: environment-related disease 25, *26*; eviction issues 22–3; Mahila Milan 122–3
international donors: aid, misuse of 167–8; NGO support 109; scheme workability 10–11

interventions: action planning 80–2; aid, misuse of 167–8; catalysts in regeneration 77–80, 141–4; ethical decisions 23–7, 165; expertise led approaches 28, 164–5; improvisation, value of 31–3, 168–9; interdisciplinary work 33–6, *34*; participation benefits 30, 165–6; practical beginnings 80; prefab housing proposal 28–31; 'reverse', incremental planning 83–5; social economy, benefits of 36–40, 142–3, 166
Involve 58

Jacobs, Jane 21, 157–8
Jayaratne, K.A. (Jaya) 107–11

Kay, John 81
Kennedy, Robert 60

Lamansk, Charlotte 67
Le Corbusier 71
'Litre of Light Project' 33
Lloyd Wright, Frank 31–2

Mahila Milan 122–3
Malecon 2000 project, Ecuador 79–80
Minton, Anna 66
morality 27

Navagamgoda (Sri Lanka): building types *113–16*, *118*; land allocation 111, 113, 117; planning options *112*; services, mixed access 117 non-government organisations (NGOs): equity, role in 65; partnerships 105, 154; Sevenatha 108

organizations, place-based 47, 106–7

participatory budgeting 58
participatory practice: action planning 80–2; communal benefits 30; communal resources 58, 77–80; decisions, approaches to 25–36, *34*; definition 60; efficiencies, appliance of 57–9; equality, promotion of 59–60, 92; governance partnerships 62–3; integrated methods 51–3; main attributes 57, 72; perceived difficulties 60–2; power holders, working with 97, 134; public/private interest 98–9; 'reverse', incremental planning 83–5, 93; roles and responsibilities (PEAS) 88–90, 94; strategic issues and value 86–8, 93–4; sustainability, related themes 45–8, *46*, *49*, 90, 110–11
peer networks 166
Peru: communal living 23–4; institutional measures 10–11
place, understanding of: informal practices 21; organizational structure 75–7, 93; participation, active processes 46–8, *49*; privatization and inequality 65–7, 92–3; social economy, benefits of 36–40; visual analysis *18*, 18–20, *20*
practice: agendas, selection of **14**, 14–16, *15*; approaches to understanding 16–17
Primary Systems Support Housing and Assembly Kits 99
prudence 163–4
public health legislation 69–70
public interest goals 98–9
Putnam, Hilary 26

rationality 25–6
reflective learning 16, 81–2
Ricketts, Aidan 98
Rockwell, David 32–3
Royal Society of Arts (RSA) 31, 57

Schon, Don 16, 81–2
Schumacher, E.F. 86–7, 156
Sen, Amartya 25–6
Sevenatha 108, 109
Slim, Hugo 163
Soil for Life 142
Solidarity 58
South Africa: food security 142; privatization and inequality 67
Special Interest Group in Urban Settlement (SIGUS) 101–6
Speight, Elaine 61–2
Sri Lanka: displacement 125–6, 135; food security 142; Million Houses Programme 102–3; Navagamgoda redevelopment 105, 111, *112–16*, 114, 117–18, *118*; NHDA's participatory framework 103–5; ownership issues 119, *120–1*, 122–3, *124*,

125; participatory practice initiatives 105–9, 108–9, 131–2; post-tsunami aid 126, *126–8*, 128–9; post-tsunami corruption? 129, *130*, 131, 136
stakeholders: active participation 47–8; analysis of priorities 83–4, 87–8; dependency on authorities 123, 125–6; partnership and governance 62–3; power holders 97, 134
Stiglitz, Joseph 59

terminology: buzzwords deconstructed *45*

terminology, deconstructed 44–5
tourism, drive for 22–3
troublemakers: negotiation 149, 156; neutralizing dissent 147–9; working with 145–7

UN Development Programme (UNDP) 22, 59

Ward, Colin 36, 67
Women's Bank (Sri Lanka) 109, 110, 125
World Bank 10–11, 25